About the Authors

Mark Phillips is a guitarist, arranger, and editor with more than 30 years in the music publishing field. He earned his bachelor's degree in music theory from Case Western Reserve University, where he received the Carolyn Neff Award for scholastic excellence, and his master's degree in music theory from Northwestern University, where he was elected to Pi Kappa Lambda, the most prestigious U.S. honor society for college and university music students. While working toward a doctorate in music theory at Northwestern, Phillips taught classes in theory, ear-training, sight-singing, counterpoint, and guitar.

During the 1970s and early '80s, Phillips was Director of Popular Music at Warner Bros. Publications, where he edited and arranged the songbooks of such artists as Neil Young, James Taylor, the Eagles, and Led Zeppelin. Since the mid-'80s he has served as Director of Music and Director of Publications at Cherry Lane Music, where he has edited or arranged the songbooks of such artists as John Denver, Van Halen, Guns N' Roses, and Metallica, and has served as Music Editor of the magazines *Guitar* and *Guitar One.*

Phillips is the author of several books on musical subjects, including *Metallica Riff by Riff, Sight-Sing Any Melody Instantly,* and *Sight-Read Any Rhythm Instantly.* In his non-musical life, Phillips is the author/publisher of a series of "fun" high school English textbooks, including *The Wizard of Oz Vocabulary Builder, The Pinocchio Intermediate Vocabulary Builder,* and *Tarzan and Jane's Guide to Grammar.* For the reference value of his numerous publications, Phillips is profiled in *Who's Who in America.*

Jon Chappell is a multistyle guitarist, transcriber, and arranger. He attended Carnegie-Mellon University, where he studied with Carlos Barbosa-Lima, and then went on to earn his master's degree in composition from DePaul University, where he taught theory and ear training. He was formerly Editor-in-Chief of *Guitar* magazine, Technical Editor of *Guitar Shop Magazine,* and Musicologist for *Guitarra,* a classical magazine. He has played and recorded with Pat Benatar, Judy Collins, Graham Nash, and Gunther Schuller, and he has contributed numerous musical pieces to film and TV. Some of these include *Northern Exposure, Walker, Texas Ranger, Guiding Light,* and the feature film *Bleeding Hearts* directed by the late actor-dancer Gregory Hines. In 1990, he became Associate Music Director of Cherry Lane Music, where he has transcribed, edited, and arranged the music of Joe Satriani, Steve Vai, Steve Morse, Mike Stern, and Eddie Van Halen, among others. He has more than a dozen method books to his name, and he's the author of *Rock Guitar For Dummies, Blues Guitar For Dummies,* and the textbook *The Recording Guitarist — A Guide for Home and Studio,* published by Hal Leonard.

Dedication

Mark Phillips: For my wife, Debbie, and my children, Tara, Jake, and Rachel.

Jon Chappell: For my wife, Mary, and my children, Jennifer, Katie, Lauren, and Ryan.

Authors' Acknowledgments

The authors gratefully acknowledge the folks at Wiley Publishing, Inc.: Tracy Boggier, Alissa Schwipps, and Jessica Smith.

Publisher's Acknowledgments

We're proud of this book; please send us your comments through our Dummies online registration form located at `http://dummies.custhelp.com`. For other comments, please contact our Customer Care Department within the U.S. at 877-762-2974, outside the U.S. at 317-572-3993, or fax 317-572-4002.

Some of the people who helped bring this book to market include the following:

Acquisitions, Editorial, and Media Development

Senior Project Editor: Alissa Schwipps

Acquisitions Editor: Tracy Boggier

Copy Editor: Jessica Smith

Assistant Editor: Erin Calligan Mooney

Editorial Program Coordinator: Joe Niesen

Technical Editor: Guy Somers
(`www.somersguitar.net`)

Senior Editorial Manager: Jennifer Ehrlich

Assistant Project Manager: Jenny Swisher

Associate Producer: Shawn Patrick

Quality Assurance: Kit Malone

Editorial Assistant: David Lutton

Cover Photo: © Brand X Pictures

Cartoons: Rich Tennant (`www.the5thwave.com`)

Composition Services

Senior Project Coordinator: Kristie Rees

Layout and Graphics: Carl Byers, Reuben W. Davis, Nikki Gately, Sarah E. Philippart, Christine Williams

Music Engraving: WR Music Service

Proofreader: Shannon Ramsey

Special Help

Alicia B. South

Publishing and Editorial for Consumer Dummies

  Diane Graves Steele, Vice President and Publisher, Consumer Dummies

  Kristin Ferguson-Wagstaffe, Product Development Director, Consumer Dummies

  Ensley Eikenburg, Associate Publisher, Travel

  Kelly Regan, Editorial Director, Travel

Publishing for Technology Dummies

  Andy Cummings, Vice President and Publisher, Dummies Technology/General User

Composition Services

  Gerry Fahey, Vice President of Production Services

  Debbie Stailey, Director of Composition Services

Contents at a Glance

Table of Contents

Introduction

*P*laying guitar is an activity that has so many terrific qualities. It's artistic, expressive, inspiring, therapeutic, and even cathartic. Nothing beats the blues like playing the blues. Guitar playing is an effective and natural means for relieving stress. But it's like sports, games, and any other physical endeavors requiring strength, speed, stamina, and coordination: The more you practice, the better you become at it. And the better you are at guitar playing, the more successful your music making efforts will be.

One of the best ways to become more accomplished in the purely physical aspects of playing guitar is to exercise your fingers — the main agents of guitar playing — to get them conditioned. And that's what *Guitar Exercises For Dummies* focuses on. By picking up this book, you've agreed to send your digits off to spring training. After going through the pages of *Guitar Exercises For Dummies,* your fingers will come out faster, nimbler, stronger, and more confident, and they'll be better team players as well. And because music involves the mind as well as the body, we give you tips and advice that will get you thinking. As Yogi Berra said, "Ninety percent of the game is half mental," so we work on strengthening your gray matter too.

In this book, we give you exercises that make sense in a musical context; that way, you learn useful things like scales, arpeggios, and chords — all of which are incorporated into the songs and pieces you play. Your brain is the coach, and the following pages are your playbook. After putting your fingers through the workout regimen of *Guitar Exercises For Dummies,* they will be lean, mean playing machines.

About This Book

Because there are real physical aspects to playing guitar, we recognize that what's true for guitar playing is also true for swimming, running, golf, or Guitar Hero: You don't get better unless you practice. And practice, in terms of the physical conditioning we talk about here, is known as *exercise.* Exercise is an efficient way for your body to practice moving specific parts in the way a given activity requires. Football players lift weights to become stronger and more powerful against opponents on the gridiron. Guitar players practice scales to become more facile at playing melodies on the fretboard.

This book is a reference you can jump into and out of at will. In other words, you don't have to read from cover to cover. Just head to the table of contents to find what you need to practice at any given moment. But it's worth noting that we present scales, arpeggios, and chords in a logical, organized way that allows you to train your fingers and learn the musical vocabulary that comes up time and again in real-life musical situations. We explain the exercise presentation most thoroughly in Chapters 3 and 4 to get you up and playing, and then in later chapters we provide more great practice opportunities but with less commentary (we can almost hear you sighing with relief). Also notice that Chapters 3 through 12 are grouped in pairs, where the first, odd-numbered chapter in the pair introduces a new concept (such as a scale or arpeggio pattern) and the second chapter has you applying that concept in a series of exercises. Both chapters in each pair include helpful exercises, but to get the most out of these chapters and be sure you can easily follow along, you may find that it's best to tackle these pairs starting with the odd-numbered chapter, where we take a little more time to explain things.

We think it's also cool that all the exercises in this book are presented in *movable* form, which means you can move them anywhere on the neck without changing the fingering, because the pattern or form uses no open strings. A movable scale, arpeggio, or chord can be transposed to any key by simply shifting your hand up or down the neck to a different starting note and playing the same pattern. So though we present these exercises in specific keys, you can move them to any fret on the neck. We remind you of the exercises' movability throughout the book, but we mention it here as well because it's an important concept in understanding how this book is organized.

Finally, most chapters end with composed pieces of music that give you a chance to play what you learn in the context of making "real music." You find these full-length practice pieces, as well as many other examples you can play along with, on the CD that accompanies this book.

Conventions We Use in This Book

Because we assume that you already play the guitar a little and are familiar with practice drills and exercises, we adopt certain conventions in this book and adhere to certain accepted terms and practices for guitar playing. For example, when we say *up* we typically mean higher in pitch, whether it's referring to a string (the high E string) or to a position. So "going up the neck" means heading in the direction of the bridge, not the nut. *Down* means lower in pitch or lower on the neck (toward the nut and headstock).

Notice, too, that throughout this book, we call the hand that you fret notes with the *left hand,* even though some left-handed people will turn the guitar over, string it in reverse, and fret with their right hand. But rather than say "fretting hand" and "picking hand," we use "left hand" and "right hand," respectively. We beg the forgiveness of southpaws everywhere.

We employ a bit of logic in the ordering of the figures presented. For example, you may notice that we introduce the major scale before the minor one. And for the three types of minor scales presented, we start with the natural minor scale. We do this because scales have a conventional order of presentation, not because, say, the major scale is necessarily easier to play than the minor scale. Also note that we always present the various patterns for both scales and arpeggios based on their starting notes — moving from low to high within a given position.

In the music figures, we introduce each new scale with a neck diagram showing you where to put your fingers on the frets and strings. The left-hand finger indications appear inside the circles (1 = index, 2 = middle, 3 = ring, and 4 = little), and the *tonic,* or name tone, of the scale appears as a white number in a black circle. The corresponding music notation is presented without bar lines. We do this to show you that it's not meant to be played in a particular meter but instead is a figure you can use to see and hear the scale without worrying about the rhythmic context. The tab staff that's presented below the figures shows the corresponding string and tab numbers, and below that are the letter names of the pitches, with the tonics circled.

Additionally, we always provide the starting left-hand finger, which appears just to the left of the first note in the standard music staff. If we offer other left-hand fingers within the figure, it's to signal that you're playing an out-of-position note, or to remind you which finger takes you back into position after having just played an out-of-position note. (By the way, an *out-of-position note* is one that doesn't fall within the four-fret span defined by the position and that requires a stretch by the 1st or 4th finger to play it.) Keep in mind that these fingerings serve as gentle reminders only. If you can play out-of-position notes using fingerings that are more comfortable or more logical, please feel free to do so. Just be sure to get back on track with the correct fingering as quickly as possible so that the following notes will be played in the proper position.

We don't provide notation for the right hand because you can play these exercises either with your individual right-hand fingers or with a flatpick. If you play with your fingers, practice the scales and arpeggios by alternating your index and middle or the middle and ring fingers. If using a pick is more your style, play the scales using *alternate picking* — playing downstrokes and upstrokes in an alternating motion, starting with a downstroke on the first note. Sometimes we tell you when a certain scale or arpeggio may favor one approach over the other, but you can play any exercise in this book using either right-hand technique. Many well-rounded guitarists play both fingerstyle and with a pick, and you're encouraged to do the same with these exercises.

You'll notice black track boxes above the music figures in this book. These boxes tell you the CD track number that the recorded version appears on. In these boxes, we sometimes include the starting time within the track. In many instances, multiple figures are included in a single track, so the timing helps to separate them. A time of 0:00 means the figure is the first one on the track.

And don't forget about the usual *For Dummies* convention that has us italicizing any important new words that you may need for the topic at hand. These italicized words are always followed by a clear, easy-to-read definition.

What You're Not to Read

One of the things we like about *Guitar Exercises For Dummies* (if we do say so ourselves) is that the music figures — which include the chord diagrams, neck diagrams, songs, and exercises — are all self-contained. That is, you can open the book to any piece of music or exercise and know what to play without reading the text that surrounds it. That's because we provide all the components you need to put your fingers on the strings and play the piece in front of you.

However, we do think it's a good idea to read the text so that you have context and a good reason for playing the figure at hand. If you decide to take the picture book route through *Guitar Exercises For Dummies* (and only look at the figures), we suggest that you start at the beginning of a chapter. This way you're introduced to each new scale, arpeggio, and chord with graphics that show you complete fingerings, letter names, and other potentially useful information.

Foolish Assumptions

Because this book features exercises — and lots of them — we decided to keep the talk brief and focus on the music. As such, we assume that you play some guitar. If you need instruction on things like buying a guitar, tuning your guitar, or playing basic chords, check out *Guitar For Dummies,* 2nd Edition.

We built this book to be played as much as read. Still, we didn't just throw you into the deep and say, "Okay, *arpeggiate* your way out of this one." We provide a basic review on holding the guitar, definitions for the notation system we use, and advice on warming up. We put a lot of music in this book, and we expect you to play all of it (eventually), so we want to make sure that you're properly prepared to spend some quality time with your guitar.

How This Book Is Organized

We organize the bulk of this book into three distinct aspects of playing the guitar: scales, arpeggios, and chords. Within each main category is a subcategory, which we call *sequences* for scales and arpeggios, and *chord progressions* for chords. Each of these pairs of activities (for example, scales and scale sequences) constitute a *part,* with the individual major and minor scales and their corresponding sequences breaking down into individual chapters. The following sections describe further what you find in each part.

Part I: Preparing to Practice

In this part, we review the skills you need to play through the book. Some material we present will no doubt be familiar to you (if you've played before). However, we also cover aspects of notation that may be new to even experienced players. So even if you don't need advice on standing or sitting with the guitar, you should check out the notation definitions in Chapter 1, especially the section on tab and rhythm slashes. In Chapter 2, we offer ways to warm up, get your head in a good place for practicing, and bolster the complementary skills of relaxation and focus.

Part II: Scales and Scale Sequences

This part begins the essence of *Guitar Exercises For Dummies,* where the rubber meets the road — or where the fingertip meets the fretboard, if you will. We start with the major scale and its corresponding sequences, and then head into the minor scale and its sequences. Besides learning the major and minor scales (and all the various patterns and corresponding sequences), in this part you also get a feel for how the book is set up. We present each scale in five patterns, and we introduce the patterns in the same order for each scale.

Part III: Arpeggios and Arpeggio Sequences

This part is where we explore the wonderful world of arpeggios — the transition point between single-note playing and chords. Technically, you play arpeggios the same way you do single notes — one at a time, just like in a scale. But with an arpeggio, you change strings more often because the spaces between the notes — which are skips instead of steps — are wider. But musically, you're really outlining chords with those single notes. So arpeggio playing is useful for getting used to how chords work in music.

Part IV: Chords and Additional Exercises

Many guitar exercise books would simply stop after presenting a healthy dose of scales, scale sequences, arpeggios, and arpeggio sequences. But that's what makes *Guitar Exercises For Dummies* so special. In Part IV, we provide the bonus material: a whole chapter on chords and chord playing. We also include supplemental exercises designed just for developing speed, strength, and independence.

Part V: The Part of Tens

If you're familiar with the grand traditions of the *For Dummies* series, you know that the Part of Tens is the fun part. It's the opportunity for the authors to take you on a bit of a side trip. In our Part of Tens, we want to give some suggestions for helping you play guitar. However, we want these suggestions to be different. We don't want to provide you with, say, ten more ways to play scales. Because much of this book is technical, we decided to discuss some ideas in a non-technical way — even if we offer advice to take up something technical (and there's a difference . . . we think). Chapter 15 focuses on ways to make your practice time more efficient. After all, we feel there's a difference between *practicing* the guitar and *playing* the guitar. When you practice, you should be as brutally efficient and serious as possible. But when you're simply playing, you should have fun. Chapter 16 is a similarly non-technical chapter. It offers ways to improve your musicianship, including activities that don't require a guitar.

Don't forget to check out the appendix at the back of this book! *Guitar Exercises For Dummies* comes with an accompanying CD that presents recorded versions of many of the figures. The handy appendix tells you how to use the CD and provides the track listing and exercise descriptions.

Icons Used in This Book

In the margins of this book, you find helpful little icons that can make your journey a little easier. Here's what the icons mean:

This icon highlights important info that comes up again and again. So read this info carefully and store it in your brain's hard drive.

These handy tidbits of info are designed to make your practice sessions easier, and they're offered at no additional charge.

When you see this icon, watch out! It points to trouble spots where you could damage your guitar or someone's ears.

Where to Go from Here

If you already have a good practice routine in place and are looking for material to start drilling those digits, skip to Chapter 3. If you find something in the written figures that you don't understand, you can always flip back to Chapter 2 for details about the notation. If you know scales already, you may want to look at the arpeggio and chord chapters, as much of this material isn't covered in other guitar exercise books.

Part I
Preparing to Practice

The 5th Wave   By Rich Tennant

"This next exercise is designed to stretch my fingers and Mona's patience."

In this part . . .

In this part, we quickly go over all the essential things you need to know to practice the exercises that appear in this book. If it has been a while since you have played, we offer a brief refresher course in Chapter 1 on holding the guitar while sitting or standing. We also cover all the notation devices and conventions that you need to be familiar with to navigate the different types of exercises presented. The material in Chapter 2 focuses on warming up. It's always a good idea in any physical endeavor (and yes, guitar playing is physical) to limber up. And because guitar playing is also a mental game, requiring focus and concentration, we give you some ways to gear up the old gray matter as well.

Chapter 1

Reviewing Guitar Fundamentals

In This Chapter

▶ Holding the guitar and sitting and standing with the guitar

▶ Understanding tablature

▶ Reading chord diagrams, neck diagrams, and rhythm slashes

*W*e know you're anxious to get started, but before you lock and load, bear down, and start drilling away on the hundreds of exercises that await you in this book, take just a moment to first ensure that you're properly set up to do the job. In this chapter, we offer a few gentle reminders regarding some guitar basics. We also provide a refresher on guitar notation. Even if you play guitar often and understand notation, you should check out the "Brushing Up on Guitar Notation" section so you understand how the written music examples in this book work.

Perfecting Your Practice Posture

You probably think we're going to tell you that you *must* practice guitar sitting on the edge of a sturdy (or, in other words, hard) chair with your back straight and your feet flat on the floor. While this posture *is* proper, the truth is that you can practice guitar in whatever position feels natural to you. After you've figured out your favorite posture, you next have to focus on holding the guitar and the pick properly. We give you pointers in this section.

Truth be told, you won't find any benefit to either sitting or standing when you practice. But it usually is more comfortable to sit if you plan to spend a long time practicing. (Most people can sit for longer periods of time than they can stand.) However, you usually stand when you perform, so it's a good idea to practice while standing some of the time.

You should hold the guitar slightly differently depending on whether you're sitting or standing. Here are the general guidelines:

✔ **Sitting with the guitar:** Most guitarists, when sitting, prop the guitar on their right leg and hold it in place with their right upper arm, which dangles over the side and allows the right hand to sweep the strings roughly in front of the soundhole (or the pickups if you're playing an electric guitar). You should pull the guitar against your body so that it's snug but not uncomfortably constricting. Make sure your right arm can swing freely from the elbow. If you place your guitar on your left leg, as many classical guitarists do, you may want to elevate your left leg 4 to 6 inches on a small stand, foot stool, or your hard guitar case so you can bring the neck of the guitar even closer to the center of your body. (Another approach is to use a device called a *support,* which lifts the guitar up while allowing you to keep both feet flat on the floor.)

✔ **Standing with the guitar:** To play the guitar in a standing position, you use an adjustable strap that positions the guitar to your body size and taste of playing. Some people like to have the guitar up high (above the belt), because this position makes playing easier. But it looks less cool. So many players like to lower the guitar to a position that doesn't seem quite so geeky. In some styles, such as bluegrass, it's okay to have the guitar up high. But rock 'n' rollers like it way down low. Of course, you should always base your guitar-positioning strategy on what feels most comfortable to you, not what's fashionable. After all, when has fashion ever involved your personal comfort?

Whether you practice while sitting or standing — or do both in equal measure — the key is to be consistent in the way you hold the guitar in each position. If you want a more thorough explanation of holding the guitar and sitting and standing with the guitar (including photographs), check out *Guitar For Dummies*, 2nd Edition.

Brushing Up On Guitar Notation

In this book, we use several notation methods for presenting the music examples and exercises. Keep in mind that you don't have to read music well to get some guidance from the notation. In fact, you don't really have to be able to read music at all if you just use your ears and listen to the CD that accompanies this book. You can get pretty far this way, but you could do better by having at least a passing familiarity with the notation conventions we use. The following sections cover all the notation systems you encounter in this book.

Decoding tablature

Tablature, or just *tab* for short, is a notation system that graphically represents the frets and strings of the guitar. For all the musical examples in this book that have a standard music notation staff (the one with the treble clef), you see a tab staff just beneath it. The tab staff aligns with and reflects exactly what's going on in the regular musical staff above it, but it's in guitar language. Tab is guitar specific, and it tells you what string and fret to play. Use the tab if you're ever unsure as to which fret or string a note falls on.

Figure 1-1 shows a tab staff and some sample notes and a chord. Here are a few points to keep in mind when reading tab:

- ✔ The lines of the tab staff represent guitar strings, from the 1st string on top (high E) to the 6th string on bottom (low E).
- ✔ A numeral appearing on any given line tells you to press, or *fret,* that string at that numbered fret. For example, if you see the numeral 2 on the second line from the top, you need to press down the 2nd string at the 2nd fret (actually, the space between the 1st and 2nd fret, closer to the 2nd metal fret wire).
- ✔ A *0* on a line means that you play the *open string* — that is, unfretted, with no left-hand finger touching the string.
- ✔ When you see stacked notes, as in bar 3 of Figure 1-1, that notation tells you to play the fretted strings all at the same time, which produces a chord. The fretted strings in the figure form a D major chord.

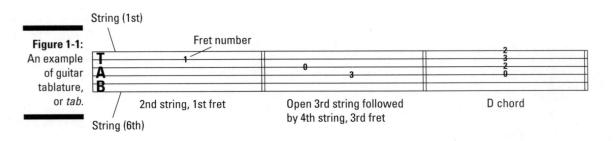

Figure 1-1: An example of guitar tablature, or *tab.*

Comprehending chord diagrams

A *chord diagram* is a graphic representation of the guitar neck that shows you exactly where to put your left-hand fingers. Figure 1-2 shows the anatomy of a chord diagram. The following list defines each of the different parts:

- ✔ The capital letter above the diagram indicates the name of the chord. Additional letters or numbers that follow define the chord's quality (minor, seventh, and so on).

- ✔ The grid of vertical and horizontal lines represents the fretboard, as if you held the guitar upright and faced the headstock.

- ✔ The six vertical lines represent the guitar strings, with the leftmost line as the 6th (low E) string. The five horizontal lines represent the frets. The thick horizontal line at the top is the nut, so the 1st fret (where you can place your finger) is actually between the nut and the next horizontal line.

- ✔ Dots on vertical lines between horizontal fret lines show you which notes to fret.

- ✔ An *X* above a string means that you don't play it. An *O* above a string means that you play it open (unfretted by a left-hand finger).

- ✔ The numbers below the diagram indicate the left-hand fingering.

Chords appearing on frets above the first four have the starting fret indicated to the right of the diagram. For example, if a chord's starting note is at the 5th fret, you see *5fr.* next to the diagram, indicating the 5th fret.

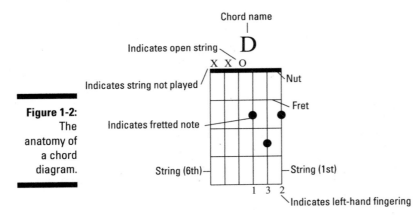

Figure 1-2:
The anatomy of a chord diagram.

Interpreting neck diagrams

In addition to presenting written music examples on a standard music staff and a tab staff, throughout this book we also sometimes show you a pattern on a neck diagram. A *neck diagram* shows several frets of the neck with the low E string appearing at the bottom. It's as if you took a chord diagram and rotated it one quarter turn (90 degrees) counterclockwise, stretched it out sideways, and then added a few more frets. The horizontal lines represent the strings, and the vertical lines represent the frets. But unlike tab, a neck diagram doesn't represent music played over time. Instead, it shows you all the notes at once.

In a neck diagram, dots on the horizontal lines tell you where to place your fingers, and the numbers inside those circles indicate which finger to use. If a dot appears in black with a white numeral, it signifies that the note is either the root (the letter name) of the chord or arpeggio, or the tonic (the note that gives the name) of the scale. Knowing the root and tonic notes enables you to identify the names of the scales, arpeggios, and chords as you move them around the neck to different starting notes. If you aren't sure of the note names on the neck, check the 12-fret neck diagram on the Cheat Sheet. All neck diagrams are accompanied by standard music and tab staffs showing the same information (and with the note names below the tab staff and roots circled), but many people find a neck diagram more useful than a staff for learning scales, arpeggios, and chords.

Figure 1-3 shows a neck diagram with the notes of a two-octave major scale pattern in 4th position (meaning that your 1st finger is located at the 4th fret). Note that the roots appear in black circles and are found on the 6th, 4th, and 1st strings. To play the scale from Figure 1-3 in its ascending form, start with the lowest-sounding note (6th string, 5th fret) and proceed note by note to the highest (1st string, 5th fret).

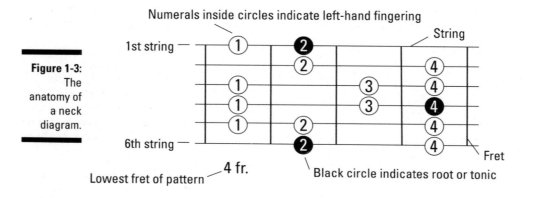

Figure 1-3:
The anatomy of a neck diagram.

Recognizing rhythm slashes

Rhythm slashes (∕) make up a shorthand system that tells musicians what chords to play and how long to play them. However, rhythm slashes don't indicate specifically what to play the way notes on a staff do. Say, for example, you see the staff shown in Figure 1-4. The chord symbol tells you to finger a D chord with your left hand. The four slashes tell you to play four strums, four quarter notes, or four beats in the style of the music that you're playing. You don't literally have to stick to four strums, one per beat, just because you see four slashes, however. You just have to be sure to play four beats' worth of music in the appropriate style. But when in doubt, four strums will be fine.

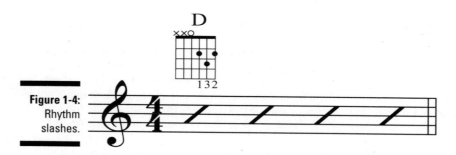

Figure 1-4:
Rhythm slashes.

Chapter 2

Warming Up for Your Practice Sessions

In This Chapter

▶ Loosening your fingers and your mind

▶ Practicing some single-note and chord exercises

You can pick up the guitar pretty much any time day or night, and you'll be able to play it fairly well. But you get the best results with just a little bit of prep work (rather than picking up the guitar stone cold and trying to wail at top speed). That preparation, which is also well-known to athletes and physical fitness buffs, is the warm-up.

A warm-up is essential for many physical activities, such as sports and playing music, because you can't play at the height of your abilities if you've recently woken from a sound sleep or have just come in from shoveling snow without gloves. You just *know* that you'll be playing better after you've had the guitar in your hands in front of the fireplace for about an hour. And no wonder. That's what warm-up routines do! They reduce the time between those states of guitar-readiness by giving your fingers the time they need to adjust to the activity at hand and play with optimum results.

In this chapter, we explore warm-up concepts for both the mind and the body (well, we limit the "body" part to pretty much the hands and fingers), and we suggest activities to try on and off the guitar. By performing just a couple of simple tasks — and sometimes just thinking about them — you can make your practice sessions a little more productive a little earlier on.

Preparing Your Body and Mind to Play

A lot of athletes will tell you that sports involve the mental game as much as the physical one. We like to think that you won't get psyched out or intimidated by your guitar, but playing music does require both physical and mental involvement. So, we consider the brawn and the brain when talking about warming up.

Limbering up your fingers

Before you even pick up the guitar to practice, you may want to open and close your hands a couple of times to stretch the muscles and tendons. Make a tight fist and then open your hands wide, splaying your straightened fingers. Then make a fist with both hands and rotate them from the wrist in a circular motion. These simple exercises help stretch out the back of the hand where a lot of tension can develop, especially when reaching out of position with your fingers or playing *barre chords* (chords where a finger covers more than one string).

If you feel like doing some more stretching, we have a few more activities for you to try. However, proceed carefully with the first two activities because overdoing any type of stretching can cause injury.

✔ **Try placing the tips of your extended fingers against your opposite forearm and press down gently to arch the fingers backward slightly.** You can do this with individual fingers by simply placing one finger against your forearm and letting the others fall forward naturally. This backward-bending of the fingers, either as a group or individually, helps counteract all that opposite-motion curling of the fingers that you do in normal playing. It's kind of like the way you might stand up tall and stretch your spine backward after stooping over for a while in the yard or garden.

✔ **Give your hands a workout by squeezing and releasing a tennis ball.** This type of ball is just the right size and springiness for guitar playing! But, if you prefer, you can grab an exercise device like a Gripmaster, which is designed specifically for working the finger muscles.

✔ **Warm up your hands by washing them in warm water.** Yup, that's right. Doing so literally warms up the hands (heat facilitates blood flow). Plus washing obviously cleans your hands, which is always a good thing to do before touching your guitar.

Reflecting on your breathing, relaxation, and focus

Just because you're engaged in a physical activity — one that requires exertion, strength, and stamina — doesn't mean you have to get all stressed out while doing it. Playing music should be fun, after all — even when you're working really hard. If you correctly approach your breathing, relaxation, and focus, you can increase your enjoyment of practicing on your guitar; plus you'll be less tired when you're finished, simply because you've successfully managed your physical and mental energies.

You don't really have to practice the mental skills we introduce in the following sections the same way you do physical ones, but you do have to be aware that breathing, relaxation, and focus are vital to improving your ability to make music.

Concentrating on your breathing

Breathing (as you might have suspected) is important. If you forget to breathe, you'll eventually pass out, and that looks very bad onstage. Seriously, though, maintaining regular, even breathing can require some thought, because often the first reaction you have when faced with a difficult challenge (whether in music or in life) is to hold your breath. But if you keep your breathing steady, the rest of your body stays in balance, leaving your other functions free to perform their duties without distraction.

A good test to see if you're breathing naturally is to check whether you're out of breath after practicing a challenging piece of music. It's natural to have some tension when trying to perform perfectly, but you shouldn't feel winded after doing so. Keep your lips and teeth slightly apart when you play. This way you'll easily be able to tell when your jaw tightens, which may be a precursor to breath-holding and other signs of tension.

Keeping tension at bay with some relaxation

Breathing naturally is the foundation of relaxation, or the state of non-tenseness that your body should be in whether you're practicing scales or playing music. While your fingers and hands are exerting themselves, the rest of your body, including your shoulders, abdomen, and neck muscles, should all be relaxed. This relaxation ensures that the energy you do need is directed at the fingers. Otherwise, that energy may be used for keeping your stomach in a knot or your shoulders scrunched up around your ears.

After you finish practicing on your guitar, try to really relax your body. Focus on each region — your chest and abdomen, your legs and arms, and your head and shoulders — and let the muscles go limp. (But don't fall out of your chair!) If your shoulders fall 17 inches as you exhale, you know you haven't been relaxing properly. In that case, you've been carrying around tension — relaxation's evil twin.

Maintaining your focus

Focus, the positive counterpart to relaxation, is an intense concentration on a particular activity. For example, if you focus on something, such as your left-hand fingers moving across the fretboard steadily and accurately, all your energies go into that particular task. Typically, the area of focus is what your fingers are doing, but sometimes it involves your eyes and brain — such as when you're memorizing repertoire or sight-reading difficult or unfamiliar music. Either way, whatever parts aren't the area of focus while you're practicing should be relaxed.

When you see confident and professional performers, they always look both focused *and* relaxed. Even when they're in the throes of an intense performance, they're having fun and their energies never seem improperly channeled. That's what focus is. It means thinking only about what you're playing and what's coming up next in the music. Focus isn't wondering what's for lunch.

Increased strength and flexibility make guitar playing physically easier over time; similarly your powers of concentration can develop so that you get better at breathing evenly, maintaining a supple carriage (the way you carry your head and body), and applying intense focus where it's needed to perform correctly, perfectly, or brilliantly.

Waking Up Your Fingers with Some Practice Exercises

The point of a warm-up is to get your hands and fingers moving on the guitar from a cold start. Physically, you're simply stretching the muscles (or muscle-tendon units) and enabling blood to flow more freely through them. You don't need to play a masterpiece to do that. In fact, you shouldn't play anything too taxing, strenuous, or complicated when warming up. In this section, we ease you in with some simple exercises that are sure to wake up your fingers better than a second cup of coffee.

Warm-ups are important, and you need to put the time in, but you don't need to devote *too* much time to them — especially if you're going to be playing scales and arpeggios as practice anyway. In that case, you can just go right to the scales, taking them slow and easy as if they are your warm-up. But, if you're going to use a separate warm-up exercise, remember that you don't have to limit yourself to the patterns presented here. Some guitarists — notably Carlos Santana — like to warm up by playing along with recorded music. Try a combination of activities and see which ones best get you pumped and primed for playing.

Single-note exercises

Single-note exercises have the advantage of getting your left-hand fingers moving one by one, which helps them to fret accurately and has you warming up with the same type of motion you use to play scales, arpeggios, and their corresponding sequences. The following figures show four exercises that each get the fingers moving in slightly different ways. You can play these exercises with a pick or with your right-hand fingers.

Figures 2-1 through 2-4 show exercises based on left-hand finger patterns that repeat for each string. The two types of movements in these four figures require going *across* the neck (which means you don't change positions) and *diagonally* (which means you change positions by going up the neck while also going across).

Because these are exercises for the fingers, there's nothing musically meaningful about them. They're all just about the pattern. So here's a hint: Look only at the tab to see the patterns more easily.

Practice the warm-up in Figure 2-1 using your 1st, 2nd, 3rd, and 4th fingers to play the first four frets on each string. Moving along the string one fret at a time, in half steps, is known as playing *chromatically*.

Figure 2-1: "Across the neck" chromatic warm-up.

Figure 2-2 shows a warm-up with a diagonal pattern. This pattern requires a shift, or a move up to a new position. Play the first four notes with the first four fingers as you do in the previous warm-up. But on the fifth note, which begins at the 2nd fret on the 5th string, start with the 1st finger so you'll be in 2nd position and can play frets 2, 3, 4, and 5 with fingers 1, 2, 3, and 4. On the 4th string, play frets 3, 4, 5, and 6 with fingers 1, 2, 3, 4, and so on. Here's a simple way to think of it: Start each new string with the 1st finger.

Figure 2-2: Diagonal chromatic warm-up.

Figures 2-3 and 2-4 show warm-up exercises that are variations on the across and diagonal movements presented in the previous two figures. Figure 2-3 places a fret in between each played note (two frets equals a whole step; thus the name "whole step warm-up"). You have to stretch a bit to play these notes, but that stretch is part of the warm-up process. Remember the battle cry of personal trainers everywhere when your fingers start to burn: "No pain, no gain."

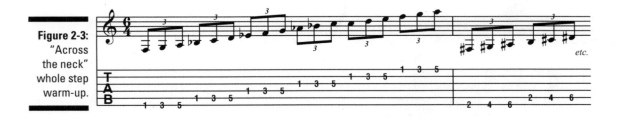

Figure 2-3: "Across the neck" whole step warm-up.

Figure 2-4 takes the whole-step stretch presented in Figure 2-3 and applies it to diagonal movement.

Figure 2-4:
Diagonal
whole step
warm-up.

Chord exercises

Playing chords is a big part of guitar, but the motion involved is somewhat different from playing single notes. The fingers each play separate strings, but they move all at the same time as you switch chords. So while single notes involve individual fingers coming into play one after another, chords involve three or four fingers all remaining still and then moving at the same time. If you're going to practice chords, it makes sense to warm up with chord-based exercises, such as the ones in Figures 2-5 and 2-6.

Figure 2-5 is an exercise using the basic major chords E, A, D, G, and C. These are sometimes called *open* chords, because they use open strings (strings that are unfretted, with no left-hand finger touching the string). Play each chord one beat apiece and focus on getting the left hand to move swiftly and accurately between changes. Don't worry so much about what your right hand is doing. Just a simple strum or pluck on the strings is fine. As you're practicing, focus on getting clear notes and clean fretting (with no buzzing or muffled strings).

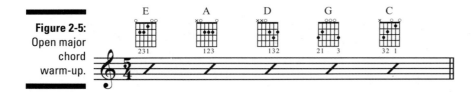

Figure 2-5:
Open major
chord
warm-up.

Figure 2-6 is a major barre chord warm-up (again starting with the basic E, A, D, G, and C chords). It's devised to get you practicing all over the neck. After you play the first measure of 5/4, notice that the progression "starts over" one fret (or one half step) higher than the starting chord. This shift upward changes the letter name of the chords in the second and subsequent measures, but you use the same chord forms as you did in measure 1.

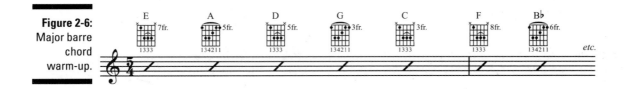

Figure 2-6:
Major barre
chord
warm-up.

Part II
Scales and Scale Sequences

The 5th Wave   By Rich Tennant

D. BOYD JAZZ GUITAR STUDIES 2ND Floor

"Okay did you feel that rhythm on the way down?
That's the syncopation I'm looking for."

In this part . . .

This is the part where we get to the meat of the music matter — scales and scale sequences. Chapter 3 deals with the well-known and beloved major scale, the staple of practice regimens that has been haunting music students for centuries. However, we present these scales in ways you can easily and efficiently learn. Chapter 4 puts these scales into *sequences,* or patterns of notes. Much of "real music" deals with scales and scale segments. Chapters 5 and 6 are the minor counterparts to the previous two chapters, balancing the happy sounds of the major scales with the more somber tones of the minor scales.

Chapter 3

Putting the Major Scales to Use in Your Playing

In This Chapter

▶ Playing major scales using five patterns

▶ Performing pieces using the major scales

Most music is based on scales. So if you learn and memorize where the scale patterns and positions are, your fingers will know what to do when you see a scale in music. Playing whole passages of notes becomes automatic.

So how do you get to such a place? By taking common scale patterns and playing them repeatedly until you know them cold. "Practice makes perfect," the saying goes, and it's true. You not only memorize the notes through repeated playings, but you gradually increase the strength and elasticity of your fingers, which allows you to play more difficult music later on. Sound like exercise? Well, it is, except that it's exercise for your fingers *and* your brain. And just like swimming, running, or biking, you need to do it several times a week to improve. For learning guitar, it's best to practice every day, even if you can manage only a little on some days.

In this chapter, you discover five patterns for playing the major scale. Each pattern has its own particular advantages, which we touch on along the way. At the end of the chapter, you get a bonus: real pieces of music to play that use the patterns.

After you memorize each fingering pattern in this chapter, simply move it up or down the neck to a different starting note to produce other major scales. The familiar *do, re, mi, fa, sol, la, ti, do* sound (think Maria Von Trapp and *The Sound of Music* here) stays the same, but, as you switch positions, the *key*, or letter name, of the scale changes. To find the correct starting note for each of the 12 major scales using the patterns, refer to the Cheat Sheet at the front of this book.

Practicing Five Major Scale Patterns

You can play major scales *in position* (meaning that the left-hand fingers cover four consecutive frets and that the position is named for the fret played by the 1st finger) by applying five unique fingerings. So with 12 major scales and 5 fingering options for each scale, you're looking at 60 major scales in position. All these options are what make the guitar so incredibly cool. You can play a lot of music by simply memorizing five patterns, and you can play it many different ways — according to the best pattern for the situation or by changing keys easily while maintaining a pattern. These options also show why you need to practice: There's a lot to master!

As you practice, play each major scale from low to high, slowly, loudly, and deliberately at first to help develop the muscles in your hand and fingers — similar to the way athletes might lift weights. Then play it faster and lighter to more closely approach how the music is actually played in performance. Just be sure to maintain your starting tempo and *dynamic level* (loudness) throughout the scale.

Major scale pattern #1

Major scale pattern #1 starts with the 2nd finger on the 6th string. The following figure shows an A major scale in 4th position in both a neck diagram and in music and tab format.

Notice that the first note of the exercise has a fingering indication in the music staff. What we're talking about is the small *2* to the left of the A notehead. This indicator tells you to use your left-hand 2nd finger to play that note. Keep in mind that the 2nd finger is actually one fret higher than the name of the position (which is always defined as the fret number that the 1st finger plays). Practice this pattern as many times as you need to in order to feel comfortable playing it.

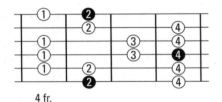

4 fr.

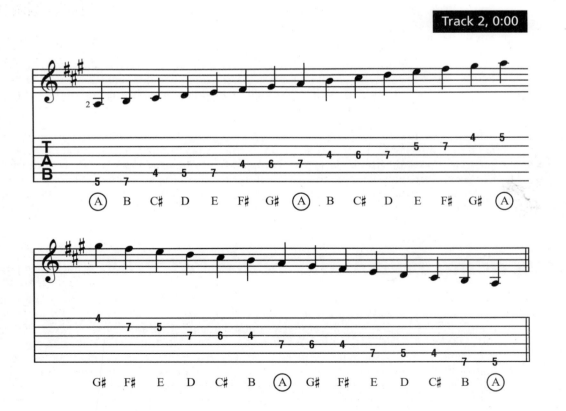

Track 2, 0:00

After you're adeptly able to finger this pattern in all keys, practice it in rhythm using the following exercise. This exercise is in the key of G major in 2nd position and in ascending and descending eighth notes. Play it in a steady beat (using a metronome or a foot tap) and try to make the music flow. The exercise may be "just a scale" but you can still make it musical by employing accents (striking the string slightly harder on certain notes, usually on the beat), and varying the length of the notes from sustained (called *legato*) to crisp and clipped (*staccato*).

Track 2, 0:35

Try major scale pattern #1 in the key of B♭ major in 5th position in ascending and descending eighth-note triplets, as shown in the following figure. In actual music (versus just scales), you encounter many different types of rhythms, not just eighth notes. So playing scales in triplets helps you mix things up a bit, rhythmically speaking. Try to give your triplets a skipping or lilting feel.

Track 2, 0:54

The next figure shows major scale pattern #1 in the key of C major in 7th position in ascending and descending sixteenth notes. This exercise brings you back to even numbers (from the triplets of the previous exercise), but the notes now come four to the beat instead of two. So play these sixteenth notes a little faster than you would play eighth notes. This way you get used to playing quickly as well as moderately.

Track 2, 1:11

Major scale pattern #2

Major scale pattern #2 starts with the 4th finger on the 6th string and includes one out-of-position note on the 4th string. An *out-of-position note* is one that doesn't fall within the four-fret span defined by the position and that requires a stretch to play. You must stretch up (higher on the neck, toward the bridge) with your 4th finger to reach this note, because it occurs one fret above where the finger naturally falls.

Wherever these patterns contain out-of-position notes, pay special attention, because these spots are where you might play a wrong note or just have trouble playing the right one correctly. If you can't perform the out-of-position note correctly, try isolating the passage with the problem note and playing it a few times by itself. Then play the whole pattern from start to finish.

The following figure shows major scale pattern #2 in the key of C major in both a neck diagram and in music and tab format. Note that in addition to the starting finger next to the first note in the music (a *4* to the left of the notehead), we include another fingering indication where an out-of-position note occurs (a *4* next to the 4th-string note B at the 9th fret). Throughout this book, we indicate fingerings for any out-of-position notes. As well, we provide the fingerings for subsequent notes if we think there's a chance you might use the wrong finger. The following figure is just such a case! Practice this pattern as many times as you need to in order to make all the notes sound smooth and effortless. When you use the correct fingerings automatically, you know you're on the right track.

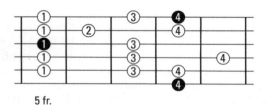

5 fr.

Track 3

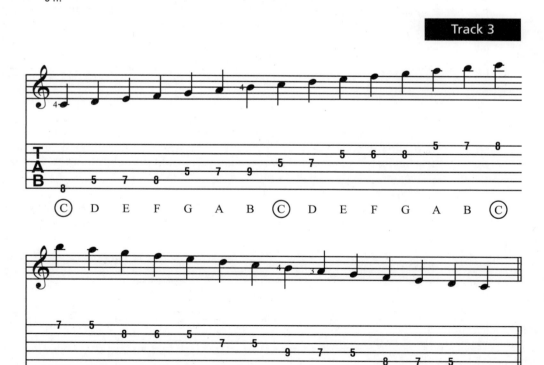

After you can successfully finger this pattern in all keys, practice it in rhythm. Here's major scale pattern #2 in the key of B♭ major in 3rd position in ascending and descending eighth-note triplets. Don't be afraid of the flats that you see in the key signature of this exercise. We know, usually guitar music is written in "guitar friendly" keys, which contain sharps in the key signature. But because you're learning patterns that can be moved around and played in any key with equal ease, a flat key is no more difficult than a sharp key or a key with no flats or sharps at all!

Major scale pattern #3

Patterns #1 and #2 have a range of two octaves, going from bottom to top. Major scale patterns #3, #4, and #5, on the other hand, span a bit less than two octaves. Playing just a single octave may seem a bit short, so in these patterns, as well as other patterns that span less than two complete octaves, we go as high as the position will allow.

The following figure shows major scale pattern #3, which starts on the 5th string (not the 6th as in patterns #1 and #2). The pattern here is in the key of D major and is shown in both a neck diagram and in music and tab format. Notice that in addition to the starting finger next to the first note in the music (a *2* to the left of the notehead), we include the fingering for the out-of-position note (a *1* next to the 1st-string note G at the 3rd fret). In this stretch, unlike the stretch of pattern #2, you reach down (toward the nut) instead of up. This move helps you get used to stretching in both directions. Practice this pattern as many times as you need to in order to feel as confident starting a scale on the 5th string as you do on the 6th string.

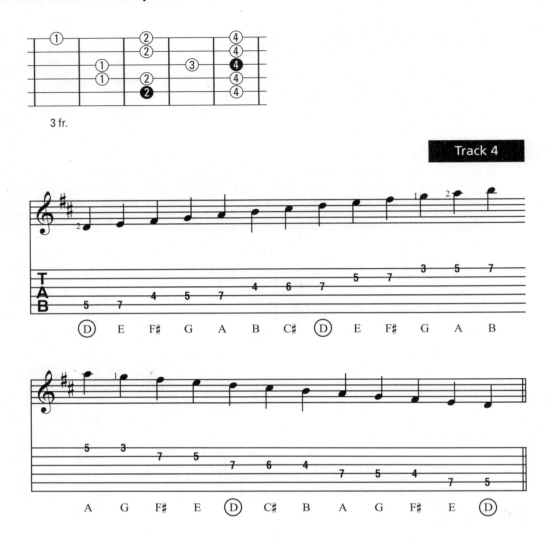

Track 4

After you can confidently play this pattern starting on any 5th-string note, practice it in rhythm with the following figure, which shows major scale pattern #3 in the key of F major in 7th position in ascending and descending sixteenth notes. Because this exercise is in sixteenth notes (which are relatively fast compared to eighth notes or triplets), play it slowly at first to make sure the notes come at a steady rate. After that you can gradually speed up.

Major scale pattern #4

Like pattern #3, major scale pattern #4 also begins and ends on the 5th string. This time, though, your starting finger is the 4th finger. The good news is that this position has no out-of-position notes (hooray!). So if you feel up to it, you can play the exercises using major scale pattern #4 with a little more *brio* (that's music-speak for speed) than the patterns that require stretches.

The following figure shows major scale pattern #4 in the key of F major in both a neck diagram and in music and tab format. Because this pattern is in the middle of the neck and has no out-of-position notes, you may want to jump right in and play a little faster. Whenever you try an exercise a little faster than you normally would, take a moment to prepare. Then play the entire exercise completely. Don't get into the habit of making "false starts," which is an indication that your fingers are ahead of your brain!

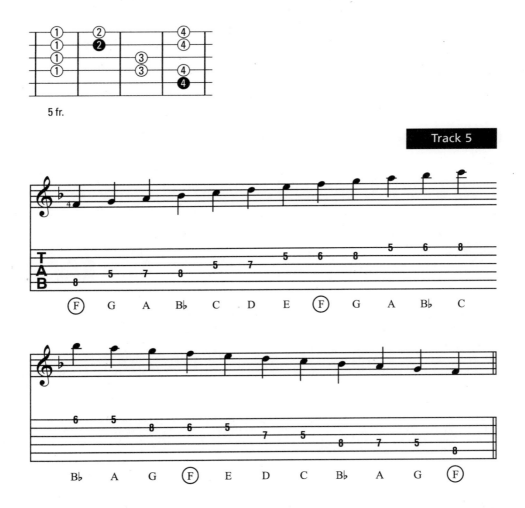

When you're ready, try the following exercise in rhythm. This figure shows major scale pattern #4 in the key of G major in 7th position. This exercise is an easy one. It's up the neck (where the frets are nicely snuggled together for comfortable playing), it's in eighth notes (which are a little easier to play than triplets or sixteenth notes), and there are no out-of-position notes to stretch for. So try playing this exercise fast from the get-go. You might surprise yourself by playing a lot faster than you think you can. Just be sure whenever you play fast that you don't rush (or play ahead of the tempo). When something seems easy, it's tempting to keep accelerating until you reach your limit. But you have to stay with the tempo established at the outset.

Major scale pattern #5

Major scale pattern #5 is a four-string pattern whose lowest note is on the 4th string. The pattern starts with the 1st finger on the 4th string, and includes an out-of-position note that occurs on the 4th string. You have to stretch your 4th finger higher on the neck (toward the bridge) to reach this note, because it occurs one fret above where the finger naturally falls.

The following figure shows major scale pattern #5 in the key of G major in both a neck diagram and in music and tab format. The stretch for the out-of-position note comes right away — on the first string you play — so watch out for it. First practice the stretch in isolation, and then try the full pattern. Play this pattern as many times as you need to in order to get it sounding as strong as the other four major scale patterns.

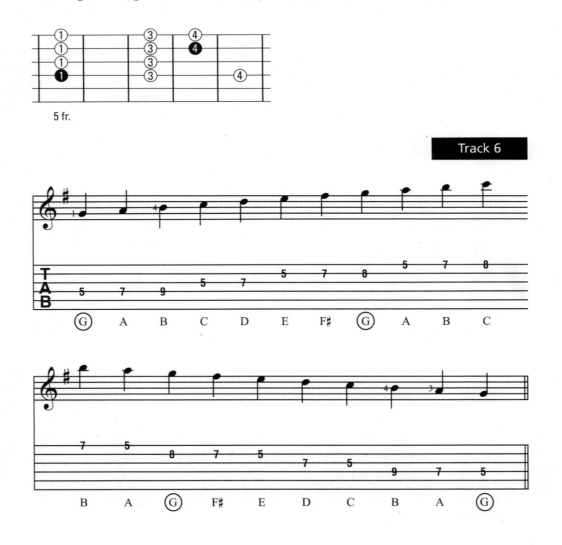

The next figure shows major scale pattern #5 in the key of A♭ major in 6th position in ascending and descending eighth-note triplets. Start with your 1st finger on the 4th string, 6th fret. Sixth position presents a moderately difficult stretch on the 4th string. If this stretch gives you any trouble, you may want to first run through the "across the neck" whole step warm-up exercise in Chapter 2.

Applying Your Scale Work to Actual Pieces of Music

Okay, so you've practiced, and now you realize that playing scales on a guitar is about as interesting as watching paint dry, right? Well, don't you drop your flatpick and grab knitting needles just yet. You've made it to the fun part where you get to use your scale-playing prowess to play *actual music* — you know, songs! It's our reward to you for all the effort you've put in so far.

After you get the five major scale patterns "under your fingers" (musician lingo for knowing them cold), you can make those patterns work for you. It bears repeating that most music is made up of scales. And although you may not encounter a lot of music that runs a scale from bottom to top and back down again in eighth notes, you will play many pieces that contain passages of scale segments — the same material you practice here. When you run across a passage that's similar to a scale you've practiced, it's like the music almost plays itself. You can go into a kind of automatic pilot and enjoy listening to the music as it goes by.

As you practice scales more and more, you'll find that playing passages of stepwise notes becomes easier and more natural. Scales are an efficient way to practice the notes contained in a song — even if the melody doesn't lay them out in a strict, regular fashion. In fact, most music isn't laid out in a strict, regular way because it would be boring and sound like, well, scales. So while practicing scales may not prepare you for a particular piece of music, it's the best way to prepare yourself equally well for most music. The following sections include two pieces of music whose melodies are made up of primarily major scale passages.

"The First Noël"

"The First Noël" is a Christmas carol that you probably know, so you can use your familiarity with it to help ensure that you're playing the song correctly — hitting the right pitches and in the correct rhythms.

You use two major scale patterns to play "The First Noël": major scale patterns #1 and #4. To begin, put your hand in 2nd position (with your left-hand 1st finger hovering above the 2nd fret). Then place your left-hand 3rd finger (your ring finger) on the starting note F♯ at the 4th string, 4th fret. Now, you're ready to play.

Take a look at the following music. Notice that at bar 8 you switch positions, jumping up to 9th position between beats 2 and 3. Try to let that half note ring for as long as possible before making the jump, but don't be late for beat 3! This mid-measure jump allows you to play the chorus of the second phrase an octave higher. The song doesn't really do that, but we thought we'd make it more interesting for you. Plus it gives you a workout in different positions.

After playing eight bars in the upper octave, shift your hand back to 2nd position at bar 16 to finish out the last eight bars. Note that the last bar, like the first pickup bar, is incomplete. It contains two beats, which allows it to even out the one-beat bar that starts the song. You can repeat the song by mentally stitching together the first bar and the last as if the whole song were a repeatable loop.

Track 7

Bach's "Minuet in G"

J. S. Bach, a classical composer who lived and wrote during the Baroque era (1600–1750), originally wrote "Minuet in G" as a simple piano piece for student pianists (a group that included his wife). Despite its simplicity, the song's melody has become universal. It even made its way into pop music in the 1965 hit by the Toys, "A Lover's Concerto."

As the title notes, Bach's minuet is in the key of G. The song begins in 9th position, and the starting note is the 4th finger. To begin, place your left-hand 1st finger hovering above the 9th fret, and then plant your 4th finger on the starting note G on the 4th string, 12th fret.

Notice that at the beginning of the music you see a *repeat sign* (the combination of thick and thin vertical lines with two dots) in addition to the usual information. In a piece of music, this sign tells you that you repeat some portion of the song. So look for a corresponding repeat sign that defines the ending and outlines the passage for repeating. In Bach's minuet, the ending sign comes at the end of bar 8. But this repeat uses *first and second endings,* indicated by the lines with "1." and "2." above the music. For music with first and second endings, you play only the first ending the first time through and only the second ending the second time through.

REMEMBER

Bach's original work has a section of music that we cut in the interest of brevity. At bar 11, the final section begins, and you switch positions so that you play major scale pattern #1 in 2nd position. The passage leads off with some string skipping, so make sure that your right hand plays the correct strings. Notice that between bar 11, beat 3 and bar 12, beat 2, three notes in a row are all played on the same fret with the same finger (the 4th) but on different strings. *Tip:* You have a choice of how to play these. You can do either of the following to play the 2nd-string note:

✔ Use the tip of your 4th finger and "hop" to the different strings

✔ Play the first note with the tip, as usual, and then flatten out your finger, forming a *mini-barre* (a partial barre that covers just two or three strings)

Many real-world situations call for the "flattening" approach, but in the case of Bach's minuet, the tempo is slow enough that you can play the notes comfortably by finger hopping if you'd like.

Track 8

Chapter 4

Adding Major Scale Sequences to Your Repertoire

· ·

· ·

*I*f you've practiced the five major scale patterns presented in Chapter 3 — and drilled them into your consciousness — it's time to have some fun with them, don't you think? Instead of going up and down and up and down (and up and down), in this chapter you get to mix things up by playing sequences. *Sequences* are musical patterns — not finger patterns like the ones you memorized to learn your scales (uh, you *did* memorize those, didn't you?).

Playing sequences not only makes practicing more interesting and less predictable, but it also makes you feel like you're playing real music — that is, pattern-based songs with repeated gestures. Many melodies get their "memorableness" from their sequences, which make them different enough to be interesting, but predictable enough to become recognizable. It's a delicate balance, but all great melodies have some repetition to them in the form of sequences, which we explore in this chapter.

Just as you did in your scale work in Chapter 3, familiarize yourself with the sequences in this chapter, and then move them up and down the neck to produce other major scale sequences in different keys. If you aren't sure how the notes lay out on the fretboard, take a look at the guitar neck diagram on the Cheat Sheet at the front of this book. It shows the letter names of all the frets on all six strings.

Practicing Major Scale Sequences

Unlike scales, which run in the same direction for long stretches, sequences change direction often, and may at first seem a little trickier than scales. But you can make them more manageable by discovering the *scheme* (or pattern), which reveals itself in the first few notes you play. Learning the pattern can help you better anticipate the direction changes and find the starting note of the new sequence. You may have to start off practicing sequences a little slower than you would scales, but you'll soon find that learning the sequence helps your brain keep up with your fingers, allowing you to play faster.

You should always play the ascending and descending sequences as a pair. In other words, always begin the descending sequence immediately after you finish the ascending one. Doing so will help you to maintain a sense of ascending and descending symmetry in your music.

Major scale sequences using pattern #1

Major scale pattern #1 is a two-octave scale that starts on the 6th string and contains no *out-of-position notes* (notes that don't fall within the four-fret span defined by the position and that require stretches by the 1st or 4th finger to play). Even though you have no stretches to contend with, you still may want to start out slowly as you play this pattern. After all, the notes change direction often and are quite different from the "one way" motion (all up, and then all down) of scale playing.

The following figure features ascending and descending four-note sequences in the key of A in 4th position. In the ascending version, between bars 5 and 6, you must use the same finger (the 4th in this case) to play two notes in a row, across two strings. This may feel awkward at first, so feel free to supply your own alternate fingering in these cases. For example, try flattening out your 4th finger into a *mini-barre* (a partial barre that covers just two or three strings), or try substituting your 3rd finger for the note played on the 3rd string. Just be sure to get back into position as soon as you can after employing an alternate fingering. And remember the old saying, "You can break the rules as long as you know the rules first."

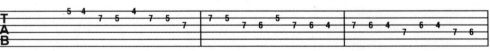

Track 9, 0:00

Following are ascending and descending sequences in the key of G in 2nd position. This exercise includes a wide skip after every sixth note, sometimes requiring you to jump over a string in the process. Practice these wide skips across two strings so you can play them with the same smoothness as you play a step on the same string. One trick that helps ensure smooth skip execution is to look ahead in the music slightly to help you anticipate the next interval.

Track 9, 0:53

Major scale sequences using pattern #2

Major scale pattern #2 starts with the 4th finger on the 6th string and includes an out-of-position note on the 4th string. Stretch your 4th finger up (toward the bridge) to play this note, as it occurs one fret above (higher on the neck) the note the 4th finger would normally play. Be sure to play stretch notes with the same smoothness as you play the in-position notes.

The following figure shows ascending and descending sequences in the key of C in 5th position. The sequences are three notes in one direction followed by a change in the opposite direction of one step. These frequent changes of direction require you to glue your eyeballs to the page to make sure you handle the twists and turns of the melodic line.

Note that in bar 2 of this figure we indicate the fingering for notes 3, 4, and 5 as *4, 3, 4* — as dictated by major scale pattern #2. In reality, however, most guitarists would play this passage with fingers 4, 2, 4. That fingering is a little easier on your hand with regard to stretching, but you have to be careful not to get out of position. When you find other opportunities in this book for alternate fingerings, you're welcome to use them. Just be sure you can get back on track for the rest of the sequence using the correct fingers according to the scale pattern.

Track 10, 0:00

The following figure shows ascending and descending sequences in the key of B♭ in 3rd position. These sequences contain no skips and are in sixteenth notes, so try playing them at a fairly brisk clip. Just because you're *practicing* these sequences doesn't mean you shouldn't be playing fast — even if the music is still new or unfamiliar to you. Real music is often played fast, so at times you should practice fast, too.

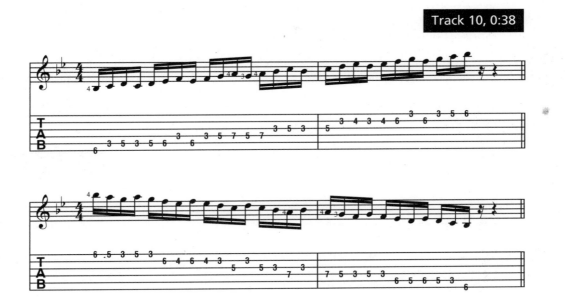

Major scale sequences using pattern #3

Major scale pattern #3 starts with the 2nd finger on the 5th string and includes an out-of-position note, which occurs on the 1st string. Play this note by stretching down (toward the nut) with your 1st finger.

Practice the following ascending and descending sequences, which are in the key of D in 4th position. This exercise starts with a skip right out of the gate — so watch out. Isolate the skip, if necessary. Beyond that, these exercises have a healthy amount of skip activity in and around the stepwise motion. It may help to memorize this pattern quickly. Then you can focus on the fretboard, which can help you play more accurately the mixture of skips and steps.

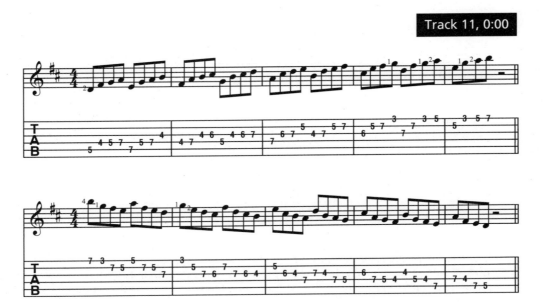

The following figure shows ascending and descending sequences in the key of F in 7th position.

There's only one skip in this sequence, which occurs immediately at the beginning. So work on speed and smoothness by playing at brighter tempos. In the ascending version in bar 2, consider an alternate fingering, such as flattening out your 4th finger to play both notes 13 and 14 at the 10th fret. In the descending version, try the same approach at bar 1 between notes 13 and 14.

Track 11, 0:40

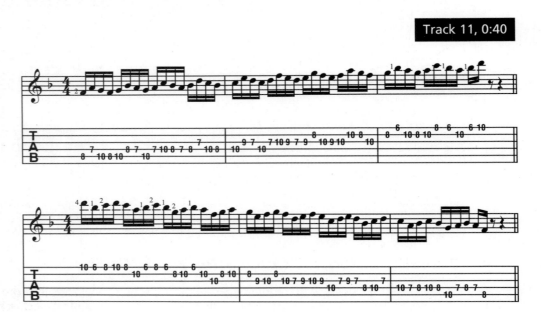

Major scale sequences using pattern #4

Major scale pattern #4 starts with the 4th finger on the 5th string, and contains no out-of-position notes. So feel free to play these exercises with a swift and light feel, if you like.

In the following figure you see ascending and descending sequences in the key of F in 5th position. Because of the way the guitar's strings are tuned (in 4ths, mostly), this sequence has many same-fret hops between strings (first seen in the ascending version between notes 4 and 5). So you have plenty of opportunities to swap out mini-barres for these cases. You have our permission to use them at will!

Track 12, 0:00

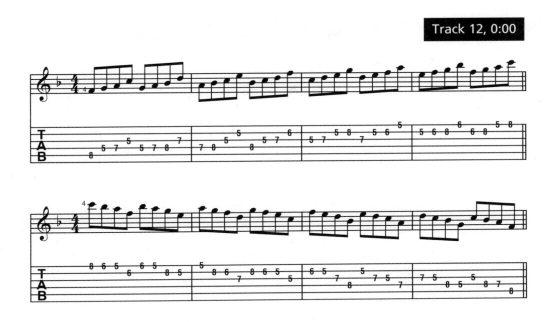

The following figure shows ascending and descending sequences in the key of G in 7th position. Only the last note of each sequence is approached by a skip (and a small one at that, a 3rd). So try playing these up to (or nearly up to) tempo right from the get-go. Playing new music fast and accurately is a skill you can develop, and this is a good sequence to try that approach on.

Track 12, 0:40

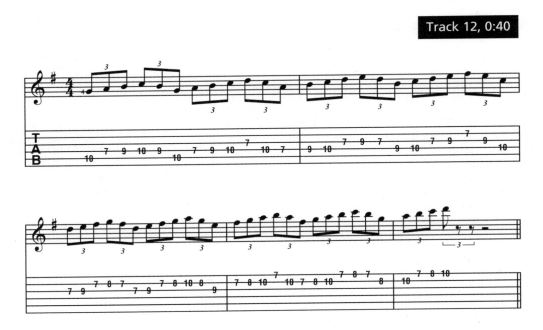

Major scale sequences using pattern #5

Major scale pattern #5 starts on the 4th string and includes an out-of-position note on the 4th string. Remember, this stretch comes right away — on the first string you play, and you have to reach up (toward the bridge) with your 4th finger to play the out-of-position note.

The figure shown here includes ascending and descending sequences in the key of G in 5th position. These sequences are fairly easy to play for three reasons:

- ✔ The same-direction nature of the melody
- ✔ The absence of skips
- ✔ As luck would have it, the lack of any same-fret string-hopping situations.

Put your metronomes on *presto* — if you dare!

Track 13, 0:00

The following figure shows ascending and descending sequences in the key of B♭ in 8th position. This sequence has just one skip, but it occurs immediately — between the first and second notes. You can breathe easy after that, however, because the remaining notes are stepwise, including the note that connects one sequence to the next.

Track 13, 0:28

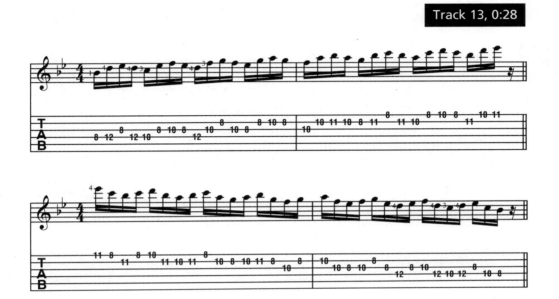

Putting Your Sequence Skills to Work with a Few Songs

The two pieces introduced in the following sections feature melodies that are based on sequences. In these songs, you'll also see scalar passages. After all, most music that contains sequences also includes scale-like material. But don't think of these songs as exercises or sequences. They're songs! Sure you're supposed to practice them, but the idea is to have fun while doing it. Simply recognizing that these songs are made up of sequences will increase your appreciation of them, deepen your understanding of their structure, and make them easier to play.

"Oh, Them Golden Slippers"

When you look at the beginning of the music for "Oh, Them Golden Slippers," notice the elements that give you clues to the song's character: tempo marking, time signature, key signature, and dynamics. (Refer to *Guitar For Dummies,* 2nd Edition, if any of these elements are unclear to you.)

"Oh, Them Golden Slippers" has two parts, and you may recognize the first part as the melody to the children's song "Polly Wolly Doodle All the Day." This children's song actually derives its melody from the early American folk song about valuable footwear.

"Oh, Them Golden Slippers" is played in A major, starting with major scale pattern #2 in 2nd position. (If you need a refresher on any of this information, refer to Chapter 3.) This song uses two scale patterns, one for each section. Use major scale pattern #2 for the first section, and remember that it has one out-of-position note occurring on the 4th string. Use pattern #1 (and enjoy the fact that it contains no out-of-position notes) for the second section, which begins after the second ending. Also, note that because the first section of "Oh, Them Golden Slippers" is played down the neck (in the lower frets), the frets are wider, making stretches a little more difficult.

A difficult stretch occurs in bar 5, beat 4, where you have to reach out of position to play the 4th string, 6th fret (G♯). Make sure you can get back into position for the next note — the 3rd string, 2nd fret (A) — which is the last note of the bar.

At the second ending of the first section, the music has a quarter rest at the end of the bar. You can use this rest as a way of silently switching positions for the next section, which is played using major scale pattern #1 in 4th position.

Track 14

"We Wish You a Merry Christmas"

As you know, "We Wish You a Merry Christmas" is a well-known Christmas carol. We didn't choose this song because we're in a holiday mood, but rather because it's such a great example of a sequential melody. When you look at the music provided in this section, you'll notice that the sequences present themselves in neat little two-bar phrases right from the beginning.

"We Wish You a Merry Christmas" is played in the key of F, using major scale pattern #5 in 3rd position. From bar 3 to 4 and in bar 8, there's some 1st-finger string hopping, but the real challenge occurs in bars 5 and 6, where the 3rd finger really has to leap around.

At the position change in bar 9 (to major scale pattern #4 in 5th position), you may notice that you don't actually have to release your 4th finger to play the first note dictated by the new position's fingering (the C at the 3rd string, 5th fret). So you can actually change positions after the text in the score tells you to. Little tricks like these help guitarists to play more *legato* (smoothly) where the notes connect or blend into one another slightly (versus *staccato,* where the notes sound separated and slightly choppy). These tricks also help musicians find economy in their hand movements that may not always be written into the music.

Track 15

Chapter 5

Tackling the Three Minor Scales

● ●

In This Chapter

▶ Practicing natural, melodic, and harmonic minor scales using five patterns

▶ Performing pieces using the three minor scales

● ●

*E*ven though major scales rule the cosmos (see Chapters 3 and 4), life would be pretty dull without their darker counterparts — minor scales. Minor scales and minor keys are sometimes described as "sad," "foreboding," "mysterious," "haunting," and "creepy." But minor scales can also be quite beautiful, and most music — even if it's in a major key — uses some minor material to convey a richer message.

As a guitar student studying and perfecting scales, you have three different versions of minor scales that you must tackle. With the major scale, you have only one. The three minor scale flavors are called *natural, melodic,* and *harmonic.* They all have the characteristic "mournful" quality, which is characterized by the flatted 3rd degree (meaning, the third note of the scale is a half-step lower than in the major scale). However, some of their other notes are altered (namely, the 6th and 7th degrees of the scale), depending on the musical context. Each of the three pieces at the end of this chapter explores a different minor scale. For now, though, don't worry about altered degrees and such; just focus on getting the notes under your fingers. This chapter helps you do exactly that!

If you're looking for even more practice, remember that after you memorize each scale's fingering pattern you can simply move it up or down the neck to different starting notes to produce and practice other minor scales. That way, you can hear how the minor scale sounds in all 12 keys using just one pattern — instead of learning 11 new ones! To find the correct starting note for each minor scale, refer to the Cheat Sheet.

Familiarizing Yourself with Natural Minor Scales

Even though a minor scale produces a decidedly different musical mood than a major scale, you treat it the same way when you sit down to practice. It's not like you have to be nicer to a minor scale because it seems so gloomy. Approach minor scales with the same vigor and positive attitude as major scales; they can take it, trust us!

Seriously, though, as far as placing your fingers on the frets and playing your right hand in rhythm, minor scales are no different from major scales. The only wrinkle is that there are three different types of minor scales (compared to just one major scale), so you have more information to keep track of. And that means you might have to spend a little more time memorizing these scales.

Compared to the major scale (the familiar do, re, mi, fa, sol, la, ti, do, or playing from C to C using all white notes on the piano), the natural minor scale has three notes that are different: the 3rd, the 6th, and the 7th degrees. These notes are *flatted,* or lowered a half step. So a C natural minor scale would be C, D, E♭, F, G, A♭, B♭, C.

Play each natural minor scale pattern slowly, loudly, and deliberately at first to build strength and confidence in your fingers. Then try playing it faster and lighter to better simulate how you'll play minor scales in actual pieces of music. Just be sure to maintain your starting tempo and dynamic level (loudness) throughout each scale.

Natural minor scale pattern #1

Natural minor scale pattern #1 starts with the 1st finger on the 6th string. As you play this scale pattern, watch for the out-of-position note that occurs on the 4th string. (An *out-of-position note* is a note that doesn't fall within the four-fret span defined by the position and that requires a stretch by the 1st or 4th finger to play it.) You must stretch up (toward the bridge) with your 4th finger to reach this note, because it occurs one fret above (higher on the neck) where the finger naturally falls.

The following figure shows an A natural minor scale in 5th position in both a neck diagram and in music and tab format. Take a look at the standard notation for a moment to see that we indicate both the starting finger (a *1* at the first note for the 1st finger) and the fingering for the out-of-position note (a *4* next to the B on the 4th string, 7th fret). Use the figure to memorize this scale's fingering pattern, and then practice it until you feel comfortable playing it. Practice this pattern several times slowly to make sure you can hear the notes that produce the minor quality as well as to get your fingers comfortable with playing a new scale.

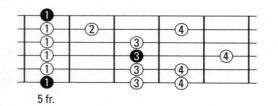

5 fr.

Track 16

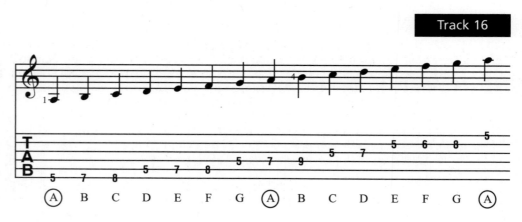

G F E D C B Ⓐ G F E D C B Ⓐ

Now try your hand at the following exercise in rhythm, which is in the key of B minor in 7th position.

Be sure not to unduly emphasize the out-of-position note (4th string, 11th fret). Some guitar players fall into the bad habit of musically stressing the difficult parts, such as stretches and position shifts. The out-of-position note here is like any other note in the scale and should blend in. The listener shouldn't be aware that the guitarist is doing something difficult.

Natural minor scale pattern #2

Natural minor scale pattern #2 starts with the 4th finger on the 6th string and includes an out-of-position note on the 1st string. Because this note occurs one fret below (lower on the neck) where the finger naturally falls, you must stretch down (toward the nut) with your 1st finger to reach it.

Here you find the neck diagram and corresponding music and tab for natural minor scale pattern #2 in the key of C minor. Notice that in the standard notation we include both the starting finger (4th finger) and the fingering where the out-of-position note occurs (a *1* next to the A♭ on the 1st string, 4th fret). Practice this pattern so you can play the out-of-position note as smoothly as you play the other notes of the scale.

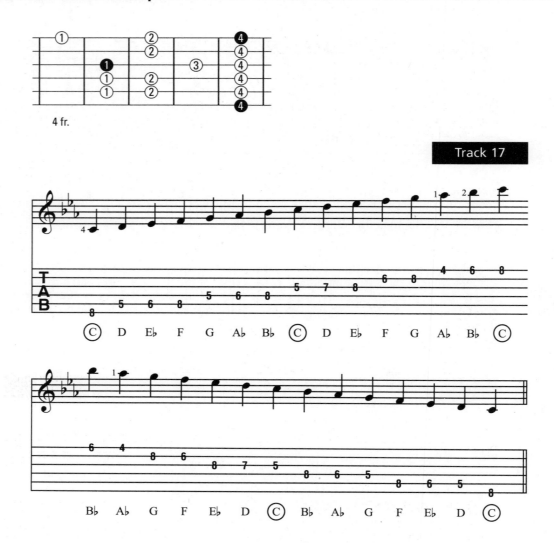

Track 17

When you're ready, try playing this pattern in rhythm. The following exercise is in the key of A minor in 2nd position. Notice that the out-of-position note occurs on the F on the 1st string, 1st fret. Because this stretch occurs low on the neck, where the frets are wider, you really have to have your left hand warmed up. Try isolating the passage that occurs between bar 1, beat 4, and bar 2, beat 2, and play it eight times, or until you get used to the stretch.

Chapter 5: Tackling the Three Minor Scales

Natural minor scale pattern #3

Natural minor scale pattern #3 starts with the 1st finger on the 5th string (not the 6th, as in the previous two patterns) and includes no out-of-position notes. Sometimes it takes a little more "aim" to place a finger on the 5th string because it's an inside string (that is, not on the edge of the neck like the 6th string, which is easier to find by feeling your way around). So just before you're ready to put your finger down, make sure you're eyeballing that 5th string!

In the following figure, we provide the neck diagram and corresponding music and tab for natural minor scale pattern #3 in the key of D minor. Because this pattern includes no out-of-position notes — which can slow you down because they take extra effort — you can try taking this pattern a little faster than you normally would. Be careful not to rush it and make mistakes, though. Practice this pattern until you feel you know it well enough to play it in a steady tempo, with no mistakes.

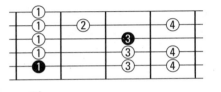

5 fr.

Track 18

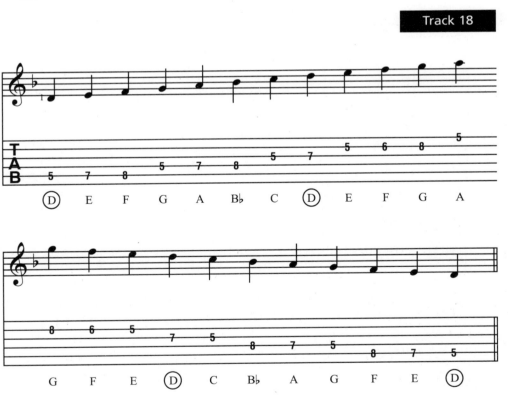

Now try this rhythm exercise in the key of E minor in 7th position. Be sure to play the sixteenth notes evenly and smoothly at first. Then, if you like, try *accenting* (striking slightly harder) the first note of each beat group. Applying accents helps to delineate the beat, which adds drive to your music.

Natural minor scale pattern #4

Natural minor scale pattern #4 starts on the 5th string with the 4th finger and includes an out-of-position note on the 1st string.

In the following figure, you can see the neck diagram and corresponding music and tab for natural minor scale pattern #4 in the key of F minor. Notice that in the standard notation, in addition to the starting finger (4th finger), we put in the fingering where the out-of-position note occurs (a *1* next to the A♭ on the 1st string, 4th fret).

You may find it difficult at first to lead off a scale with the 4th finger, because it's traditionally a weaker and "less confident" finger than the 1st (the finger that begins natural minor scale patterns #1 and #3). So practice the beginning of this pattern (just the first three or four notes) a few times to make sure you kick it off steadily and confidently before playing the rest of the pattern.

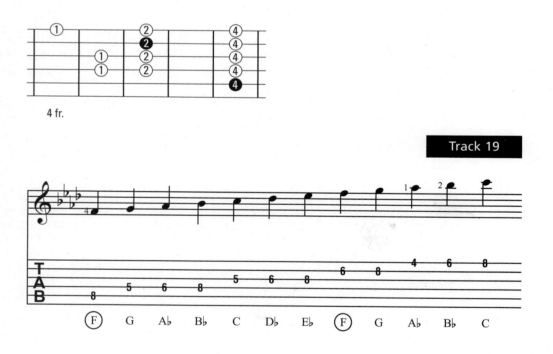

Track 19

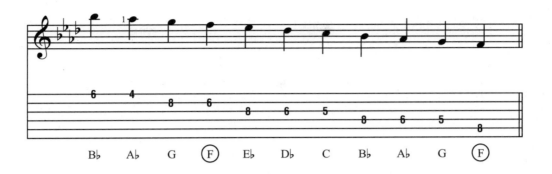

B♭ A♭ G (F) E♭ D♭ C B♭ A♭ G (F)

When you're ready to try this pattern in rhythm, check out the following figure, which is in the key of D minor in 2nd position. In this rhythm exercise, notice that an out-of-position note occurs on the F on the 1st string, 1st fret.

A stretch to the 1st fret is a wide one, so try measuring it first by placing your 4th finger on the 2nd string, 5th fret. While still holding your 4th finger down, reach up and place your 1st finger on the 1st string, 1st fret, and hold that down, too. That's the span your hand will have to make when you encounter the reach in bar 2. This measuring routine should help you remember how far to stretch when the time comes, and it's a little quicker than isolating the passage containing the stretch.

Natural minor scale pattern #5

Natural minor scale pattern #5 starts with your 1st finger on the 4th string and includes no out-of-position notes.

Refer to the following figure to see the neck diagram and corresponding music and tab for natural minor scale pattern #5 in the key of G minor. Because this pattern begins on an inside string (away from the easily accessible edges of the guitar), you may want to practice placing your 1st finger quickly on the starting note. The good news is that you're back to beginning a scale with a strong finger — the 1st. Practice grabbing the starting note at different points on the neck, naming each starting note as you do, and then play through the pattern at least four times to memorize the fingering.

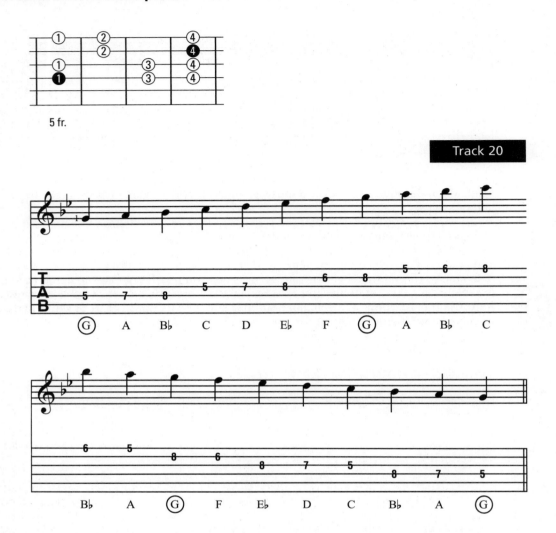

The following figure provides a rhythm exercise in the key of A minor in 7th position. To help emphasize the sound of a triplet, play the first note in each group of three with a slight accent — that is, strike it a little harder than you do the surrounding notes.

Raising the Bar with Melodic Minor Scales

Compared to the major scale (for example, C, D, E, F, G, A, B, C in the key of C), the ascending melodic minor scale has one note that's different: the 3rd, which is flatted. So an ascending C melodic minor scale would be C, D, E♭, F, G, A, B, C. The descending melodic minor is the same as the natural minor scale, and so it has three notes that are different: the 3rd, 6th, and 7th degrees. These are flatted, so a descending C melodic minor scale would be C, B♭, A♭, G, F, E♭, D, C.

The raising of the notes on only the ascending version is said to make the scale more elegant. Much Baroque and Classical music — undoubtedly elegant — often includes melodic minor scales.

Because the sixth and seventh notes are sometimes raised and sometimes not, the melodic minor scale can be somewhat tricky to memorize. But that difficulty is also what makes it interesting. After all, you simply have more notes available than with the other major and minor scales. Practice the melodic minor scale as you would the natural minor scale, but do be aware of the two scale degrees that are different (the 6th and 7th) on the ascending version. Don't make these notes obvious by hitting them harder, either. Give the raised and unraised notes equal emphasis.

Melodic minor scale pattern #1

Melodic minor scale pattern #1 begins on the 6th string with the 1st finger.

The upcoming figure shows the neck diagram and corresponding music and tab for the pattern. Because the melodic minor scale has two forms — one for ascending and one for descending — we include two neck diagrams side by side.

The ascending form of the melodic minor scale pattern #1 includes out-of-position notes on the 5th, 4th, and 2nd strings. The descending form includes just one out-of-position note, on the 4th string. We indicate the fingerings for these notes in the standard notation. Between the ascending and descending versions you have a fair amount of stretching to do here, so make sure you're limbered up before trying this one!

Because only the top part of the scale (between the 6th and octave note) presents the raised and unraised notes, you need to isolate the passage from the high E (2nd string, 5th fret) to the high A (1st string, 5th fret), ascending and descending. Play the passage eight times in a row at a slow tempo before trying the exercise from the beginning. As you memorize the scale, make sure your fingers don't get confused as to which notes they're supposed to play on the ascent versus the descent. Practice this pattern both up and down so you memorize the difference between the two versions of the scale.

Ascending

Descending

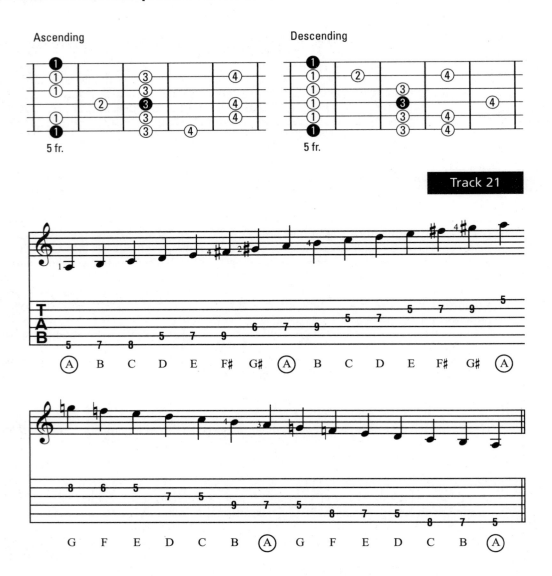

Track 21

Here's an exercise in rhythm in the key of G minor in 3rd position. Play the eighth notes with a light and quick feel, just as you would with the natural minor scale, and work so that you can negotiate the altered notes here with equal ease.

The melodic minor scale is different on the way down. So if you've become used to coasting on the descending versions of other scales, you'll have to pay more attention here!

Melodic minor scale pattern #2

Melodic minor scale pattern #2 starts with the 4th finger on the 6th string and includes two out-of-position notes. One of these notes occurs when ascending (on the 4th string) and one occurs when descending (on the 1st string).

The following figure shows the neck diagrams in ascending and descending forms along with the corresponding music and tab for melodic minor scale pattern #2 in the key of C minor. Notice that in the standard notation, in addition to the starting finger (4th finger), we put in the fingerings where the out-of-position notes occur. So not only is the scale different depending on the direction you're going, but the out-of-position notes change as well. Melodic minor scales are really two scales under one name. That means two times the effort to learn, but two times the possibilities for musical variety! Practice this pattern along with natural minor scale pattern #1, if you want; they're identical in their descending versions.

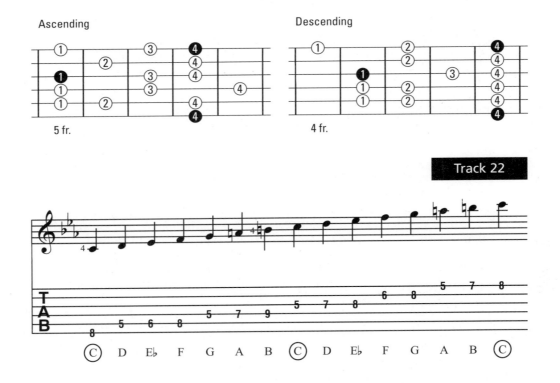

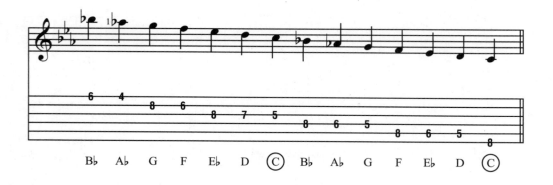

Bb   Ab   G   F   Eb   D   (C)   Bb   Ab   G   F   Eb   D   (C)

After you have the pattern down pat, use the rhythm exercise shown in the following figure as practice. This exercise is in the key of B minor in 4th position.

Melodic minor scales require you to think, stretch, and keep track of which 6th and 7th degrees to use. Are you staying relaxed through this process? Don't tense up, even if you have to stretch your fingers and think fast to ensure correctly played notes. And whatever you do, keep breathing!

Melodic minor scale pattern #3

Melodic minor scale pattern #3 starts with the 1st finger on the 5th string. The ascending form contains an out-of-position note on the 4th string. You must stretch up (toward the bridge) with the 4th finger to play this note. The descending form, which is the same as natural minor scale pattern #3, contains no out-of-position notes.

Here you find the neck diagrams as well as the corresponding music and tab for this scale pattern in the key of D minor in both ascending and descending forms. Note the unusual stretch here: You play the out-of-position note with the 4th finger, but the next note is played with the 2nd finger (not the 1st, as you may expect). Stretching between the 4th and 2nd fingers is a little more difficult than between the 4th and 1st fingers, so practice the move from the 4th to the 3rd string two or three times before playing the entire pattern.

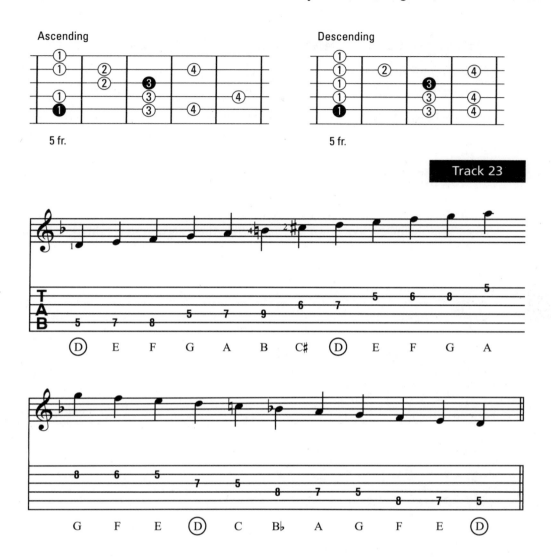

Ready to put this pattern into play? If so, check out this exercise, which is in the key of F♯ minor in 9th position. Playing this scale higher up the neck ensures that the stretch you encounter from playing the out-of-position notes is made a little easier because the frets are closer together. So if you have any say in the matter, always opt to head north to play this scale. Your fingers will thank you for it.

Melodic minor scale pattern #4

Melodic minor scale pattern #4 starts with the 4th finger on the 5th string and includes an out-of-position note on the 1st string in both the ascending and descending forms.

To see the neck diagrams and corresponding music and tab (in ascending and descending forms) for melodic minor scale pattern #4 in the key of F minor, check out the following figure. Because the stretch occurs in the same place in both the ascending and descending versions, do a quick hand-span measurement (which is discussed in the earlier section "Natural minor scale pattern #4") between the 2nd and 1st strings at the 8th and 4th frets, respectively. Then you can jump into the pattern. Watch out for the notes on the 3rd and 2nd strings, though. They're different, depending on which direction you're traveling. Practice this pattern a few times, or until you can play the ascending version as easily as the descending version (which is the same as natural minor scale pattern #4, a scale we discuss earlier in the chapter).

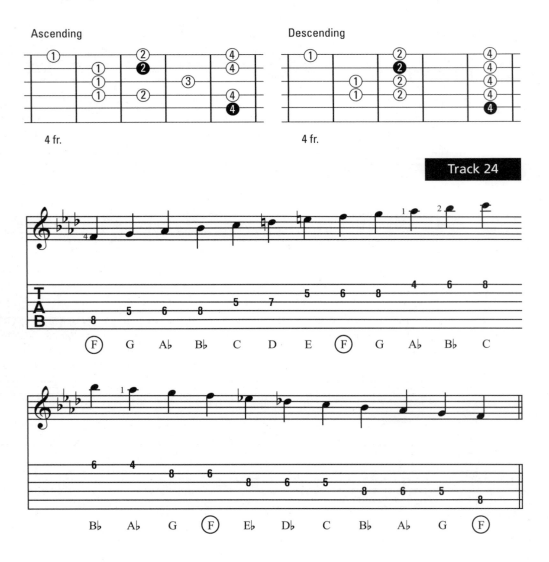

Now take a look at the following figure, which provides a rhythm exercise in the key of E minor in 4th position. Notice that an out-of-position note occurs on the G on the 1st string, 3rd fret. As melodic minor scales go, this pattern is relatively accessible, because its stretch occurs in only one spot (on the 1st string). Practice the stretch first to get your fingers limbered up, and then focus on the differences between the ascending and descending versions, which requires a limber brain.

Melodic minor scale pattern #5

Melodic minor scale pattern #5 begins with the 1st finger on the 4th string and includes no out-of-position notes in either the ascending or descending versions.

In the following figure, you can see the neck diagram and corresponding music and tab in ascending and descending form for melodic minor scale pattern #5 in the key of G minor. Use the figure to memorize this scale's fingering pattern, and then practice it several times to ensure that the notes are equally smooth and even in either direction.

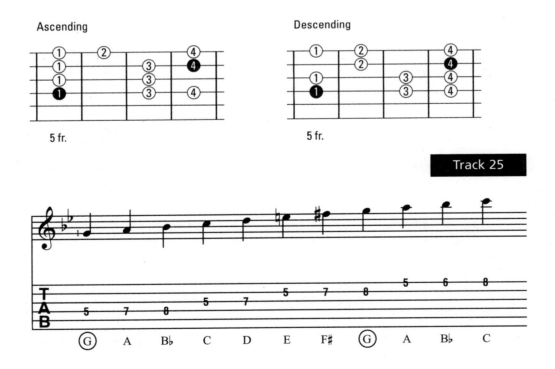

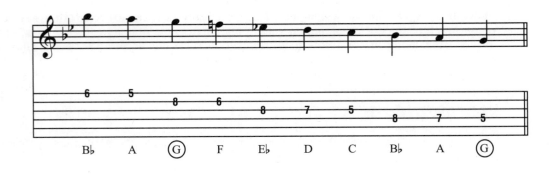

When you have pattern #5 memorized, use the following figure to practice it in rhythm. This exercise is in the key of B♭ minor in 8th position.

B♭ minor is an unusual key for the guitar, because it contains five flats. Guitarists generally find themselves in sharp keys (such as G, D, A, and E), which are considered more favorable to the instrument. (This relates to the open strings of the guitar being the tonics, or starting notes, of sharp keys.) And when guitar players do have to play in flat keys, they're more comfortable with keys that have only a few flats (such as F, B♭, and E♭, which have one, two, and three flats, respectively). But one of the advantages of movable scale patterns is that they let you explore uncharted territory (including keys with lots of flats) without having to learn any new patterns.

Harmonizing with Harmonic Minor Scales

Compared to the major scale, the harmonic minor scale has two notes that are different: the 3rd and the 6th degrees. These are flatted, so a C harmonic minor scale would be C, D, E♭, F, G, A♭, B, C.

Consider the harmonic minor scale alongside its other minor scale brethren. The harmonic minor is different from the natural minor in that the 7th degree is raised a half step. This is true whether the scale is ascending or descending. This raising of the 7th degree gives the scale's melody a strong pull from the 7th degree to the top of the scale. It also allows for the formation of a dominant seventh chord in the harmony (for example, an E7 chord in the key of A minor). For these reasons, the scale is called the "harmonic" minor. After all, it allows more desirable chords to be formed from it.

Raising the 7th degree produces a colorful "skip" in the melody between the unraised 6th and the raised 7th. Some people think this skip isn't very scale-like, but the harmonic minor has a tart flavor and sounds Middle Eastern (think snake charmer music). The harmonic minor scale is the same ascending and descending, and so it should be a little easier to memorize than the melodic minor scale. Practice all five patterns of the harmonic minor scale until you can play them as smoothly — skip and all — as you do the natural and melodic minor scales.

Harmonic minor scale pattern #1

Harmonic minor scale pattern #1 is shown here as an A harmonic minor scale in 5th position, starting with the 1st finger on the 6th string.

The following figure shows the neck diagram as well as the corresponding music and tab. This pattern has out-of-position notes on the 4th and 2nd strings. We include fingerings for these notes in the standard notation. The stretch that occurs on the 2nd string, between the 2nd and 4th fingers, is unusual, so practice playing just the second string notes two or three times before playing the rest of the pattern. Keep in mind that you have another stretch to contend with, too — on the 4th string between the 3rd and 4th fingers. But this is the kind of stretch you're used to, so it shouldn't present an additional problem, as long as you're prepared for it.

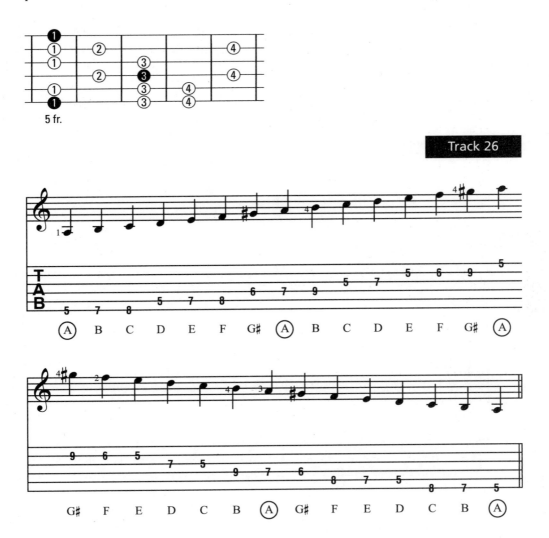

Try the rhythm exercise in the following figure, which is in the key of C minor and in 8th position. Before you begin playing, notice where the out-of-position notes fall, and be sure to observe the fingering indications.

As an option, you can play fingers 1, 2, and 4 on the 4th string (instead of fingers 2, 3, 4). This eliminates the stretch that occurs between the 3rd and 4th finger, which some people find uncomfortable.

Harmonic minor scale pattern #2

Harmonic minor scale pattern #2 starts with the 4th finger on the 6th string, and it includes out-of-position notes on the 4th and 1st strings. You stretch up (toward the bridge) with the 4th finger to reach the out-of-position note on the 4th string, and you stretch down (toward the nut) with the 1st finger to reach the out-of-position note on the 1st string.

The following figure shows the neck diagram and corresponding music and tab for harmonic minor scale pattern #2 in the key of C minor. In the standard notation, in addition to the starting finger (4th finger), we put in the fingerings where the out-of-position notes occur. Use these figures to familiarize yourself with the fingering pattern, and then play it until you know it cold.

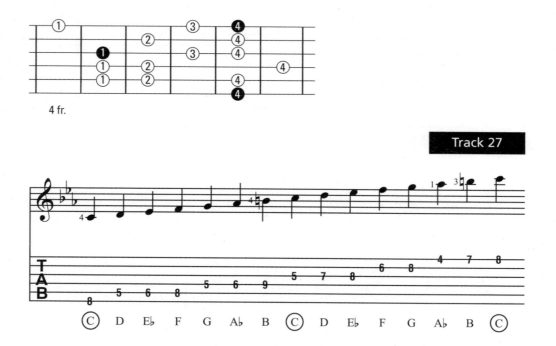

B A♭ G F E♭ D Ⓒ B A♭ G F E♭ D Ⓒ

To practice this pattern in rhythm, check out the next figure, which is in the key of D minor in 7th position. Accent the first note of each triplet to help keep your place in the measure.

Harmonic minor scale pattern #3

Harmonic minor scale pattern #3 starts with the 1st finger on the 5th string and includes no out-of-position notes. Lucky you!

Take a look at the following figure, which shows the neck diagram and corresponding music and tab for harmonic minor scale pattern #3 in the key of D minor. Be careful that you don't overemphasize the note that's played with the 2nd finger on the 3rd string (the raised 7th). In trying to memorize the sound and fingering of the three different minor scales, it's pretty obvious that the seventh note of the scale is the one that adds the "flavor." But you should work to make the attack as even as the rest of the notes of the scale. To ensure that you aren't applying undue emphasis to any particular note, practice this pattern in its entirety every time you play it (without isolating specific passages), and work to make all the notes equal in volume.

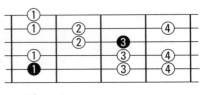

5 fr.

Track 28

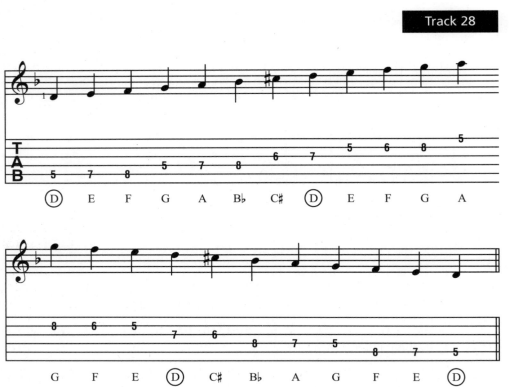

When you have pattern #3 under your belt, practice it in rhythm. To do so, consult the next figure, which is in the key of B minor in 2nd position. Playing a pattern that has no stretches and is the same ascending as descending sounds like an opportunity to give it the gas. Practice this exercise at a bright tempo, but be careful that you don't flub the notes because your fingers are going too fast for your brain. Just because you find a scale to be technically easy doesn't mean you won't make a mistake due to a lapse in concentration.

Harmonic minor scale pattern #4

Harmonic minor scale pattern #4 starts with the 4th finger on the 5th string and includes an out-of-position note on the 1st string. You must stretch down (toward the nut) with the 1st finger to play it.

This figure shows the neck diagram and corresponding music and tab for harmonic minor scale pattern #4 in the key of F minor. The 1st-finger note on the 1st string creates a two-fret stretch between the 1st and 2nd fingers. Be aware of this unusual stretch as you approach the 1st string. To limber up for the out-of-position note before you encounter it in rhythm, try practicing this pattern descending (from the top note down) first. After you do that a couple of times, practice the scale in the normal ascending approach four times, or however many times you need to memorize the fingering and feel comfortable playing the notes.

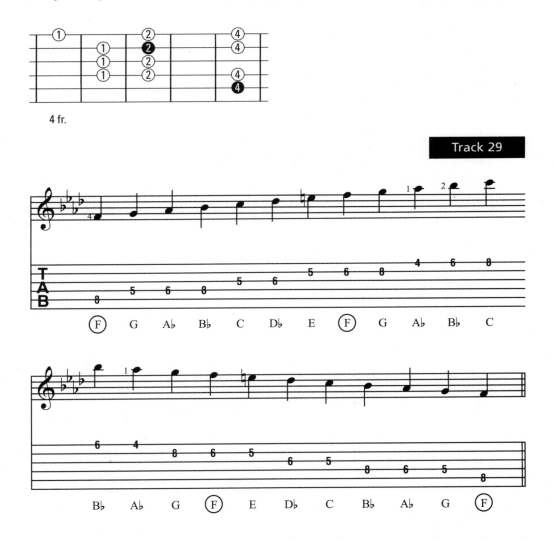

When you're ready for some practice, try your hand at the exercise in the following figure, which we've placed in the key of G minor in 7th position. When playing eighth notes in 4/4 time, the most important beat is beat 1. The next most important is beat 3, followed by beats 2 and 4. Can you play a right hand articulation approach that reflects that? *Tip:* Don't make the changes in volume between the accented notes and the unaccented ones too drastic, or it becomes harder to play an even, steady rhythm.

Harmonic minor scale pattern #5

Harmonic minor scale pattern #5 starts with the 1st finger on the 4th string and includes no out-of-position notes.

To see the neck diagram and corresponding music and tab for harmonic minor scale pattern #5 in the key of G minor, refer to the following figure. Because this pattern has no stretches to contend with, it's rather easy to play. So try doing something different: Focus on your right hand. If you normally use a flatpick, try playing the notes smoothly and evenly by alternating your right-hand index and middle fingers. Conversely, if you play fingerstyle, try picking up a flatpick for this one. (Come on, it won't kill you to do it! And your classical guitar teacher doesn't even have to know.) In either case, approaching an exercise from a different perspective often helps you solidify your own internal rhythmic sense, so that when you go back to the way you would normally play, you find new confidence. Practice this pattern using different right-hand approaches, as a way to see "how the other half lives."

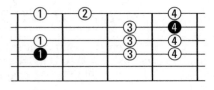

5 fr.

Track 30

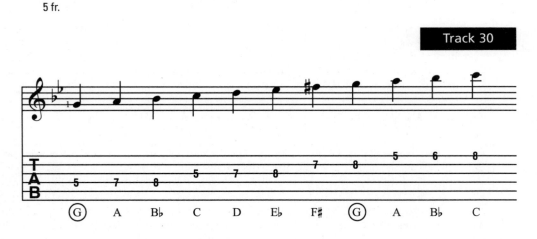

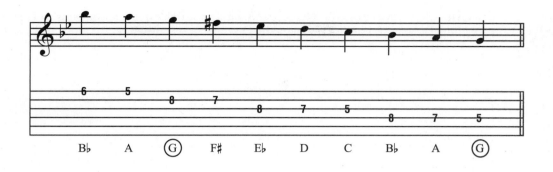

When you're ready, practice the pattern using the following figure, which is in the key of F♯ minor in 4th position. Have you ever played in the dark or with your eyes closed? It's a great way to test your muscle memory, and performing this experiment on a scale with no out-of-position notes is a good place to start. It's also the acid test for seeing whether you *truly* have a pattern memorized. Try closing your eyes right now, and see how well you do going up and down one time slowly and steadily. No peeking!

Playing Pieces Using the Three Minor Scales

Playing minor scales prepares you for the vast underworld of music that forsakes major-key optimism and chooses to express itself in darker tones. Just as you need both sunshine and rain to make your flowers grow, so too do you need a little minor amongst the major to make your musical garden flourish.

In this section, you get to see what minor-scale music is all about. We present three major-league compositions, each using a different minor scale. One piece is an old traditional carol, one is from the great Baroque composer George Frederick Handel, and one is attributed to the Renaissance. Enjoy your musical journey to the dark side!

"God Rest Ye Merry, Gentlemen"

Despite the fact that "God Rest Ye Merry, Gentlemen" is in a minor key, it's quite spirited and uplifting. Take a look at the music provided to see what we mean. The key signature has no sharps or flats, so you may think that the song is in C major. But it's actually in A minor, which shares the same key signature and notes as C major. (Now you see why A minor is known as the relative minor of C major). This song is composed of almost all quarter notes, so you can take it at a pretty brisk tempo. The song uses just one pattern, natural minor scale pattern #5, in 7th position, starting with the 1st finger.

Even though we've arranged the song using all one scale pattern, some of the intervals and direction changes can be tricky. Try playing the song by ear (close the book or look away from the music). No peeking, now! See how well you do at picking out the correct notes. Even when you know the pattern cold, "God Rest Ye Merry, Gentlemen" can be difficult to perform completely accurately because of some of the intervals.

Track 31

Handel's "Allegro"

The opening statement in this piece is just an ascending scale. However, you may not even realize it because of the way it's disguised with different rhythms. The faster notes in bars 5 through 7 are all just descending scale segments, but do note how beautiful they sound.

Handel's "Allegro," which is shown in the following figure, uses melodic minor scale pattern #4 in 7th position, starting with the 4th finger. It's in the key of G minor and written in *cut time* (sometimes referred to as *2/2*), which is indicated with a C and a vertical line "cutting" it in half (¢). This symbol tells you to count the half note, not the quarter note (as you're used to doing with songs in 4/4 and 3/4), as one beat. Because you count the half note as the beat, the measure is felt in 2 (with two beats to the bar).

In bar 3 of this piece, you see two accidentals in the music: an E natural and an F sharp. These accidentals indicate that those notes have been raised as the melodic minor commands. In bar 5, the melody descends, so the melodic minor scale again requires that the E and F — raised on the way up — be in their natural state, as F and E flat, which agrees with the key signature. For you music readers, we put in the natural and flat signs in bar 5 just as a gentle reminder not to play the wrong notes. The melody has a nice way of building here, using slow notes in the beginning and working up to the eighth-note passages in bars 5 through 7.

Track 32

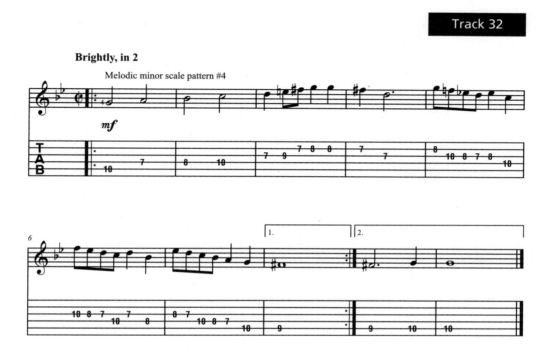

Brightly, in 2

Melodic minor scale pattern #4

"The Three Ravens"

If you're old enough, you may recognize "The Three Ravens" from the Peter, Paul, and Mary version of this folk song. The key signature in the music tells you that this song is in F minor, but because you're using the harmonic minor scale, every instance of the note E will be E natural, not E♭ as indicated by the key signature.

Because the harmonic scale here is in 1st position and you have some out-of-position notes to play, you have a pretty serious case of finger stretching ahead of you! So first play bars 1 through 3 in isolation. This bit of practice allows you to execute the stretch in both an ascending and descending context. Practicing these stretching parts ensures that they don't take you by surprise when you try to play the whole piece.

Moderately slow, in 2

Harmonic minor scale pattern #1

Harmonic minor scale pattern #3

Chapter 6

Examining Minor Scale Sequences

*I*n Chapter 5, we show you the three types of minor scales: natural, melodic, and harmonic minor. In this chapter, you put those scales into sequences. Each of the three types of minor scales has five patterns, so altogether you get to play 15 unique scale-pattern combinations.

Throughout this chapter you work with ascending and descending sequences. Try to practice the sequences as pairs to ensure that you can play both equally well. Practice each pair as many times as you need to in order to feel comfortable playing them and to ensure that each pair is as strong as any other.

Try to memorize the patterns as you play them. Doing so will help you better anticipate where the written music will take you next. And remember, until you get the hang of the pattern and fingerings used in a sequence, start slow and work your way up to speed (the way you would with a scale). And just as in your scale work (see Chapters 3 and 4), you should move all the sequences presented in this chapter up and down the neck to produce other minor scale sequences. To find the starting notes on the neck for different scale sequences, refer to the neck diagram on the Cheat Sheet; it lists the names of the notes on all six strings.

It's Only Natural: Practicing Natural Minor Scale Sequences

The natural minor scale is the most common of the minor scales, so sequences based on their scale patterns start to sound like real music. However, before playing the sequences themselves, try practicing the scale a few times. Doing so will help you remember the fingering. If at any time you find you're hitting the wrong notes of the scale (and not just a scale note out of sequence), refer to Chapter 5 for the scale exercises that correspond to these sequences.

Natural minor scale sequences using pattern #1

The following figure shows ascending and descending sequences in the key of G minor in 3rd position. Play these sequences in the same way you would a scale, working to make sure the notes are smooth, even, and flowing from one into another. To play the out-of-position note on the 4th string, stretch your 4th finger up (toward the bridge) to reach the note. (By the way, an *out-of-position note* is one that doesn't fall within the four-fret span defined by the position and that requires a stretch by the 1st or 4th finger to play it.)

Track 34, 0:00

Natural minor scale sequences using pattern #2

The following figure shows ascending and descending sequences in the key of E minor in 9th position. Play the triplets with a light and buoyant feel, and accent the first note in each group by striking it slightly harder than the others.

Track 34, 0:53

Natural minor scale sequences using pattern #3

The ascending and descending sequences in the following figure are in the key of C minor in 3rd position. You have no out-of-position notes to stretch for in this sequence, but you can make the fingering a little easier on yourself by employing a *mini-barre* (flattening out one finger to fret two or three strings simultaneously). For example, in bar 2 of the ascending version, create a mini-barre with your 1st finger as you place it across the 2nd and 3rd strings, just in time to play the 2nd string at the 3rd fret. The following note, occurring on the 3rd string at the 3rd fret, is then already fretted and waiting for you!

Track 34, 1:32

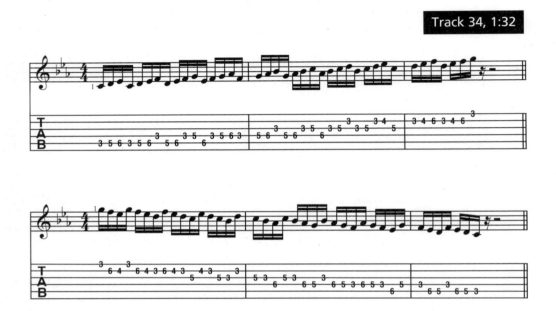

Natural minor scale sequences using pattern #4

Try practicing the ascending and descending sequences in the following figure. They're in the key of F♯ minor in 6th position. Remember to stretch downward (toward the nut) with the 1st finger for the out-of-position note that occurs on the 1st string.

This exercise offers many opportunities to employ mini-barres and alternate fingerings. For example, in the ascending version, play a mini-barre for the notes in bar 1, between the 3rd and 4th strings. In bar 2 substitute your 3rd finger for your 4th to play the 4th string, 9th fret. And in bar 3 use your 1st finger instead of the 2nd to play the 3rd string, 7th fret. Finally, in bar 4 play the first two 9th-fret notes with fingers 3 and 4, which is preferable to using 4 both times or creating a 4th-finger mini-barre.

If this seems like a lot to follow, don't worry. Take each one by itself and write the fingering in the music itself (lightly and with a pencil!) the way teachers have been doing in students' lesson books since the dawn of guitar lessons. Keep in mind, you don't have to employ all or any of these suggestions, but they're there for you to try anytime you like.

Track 34, 2:08

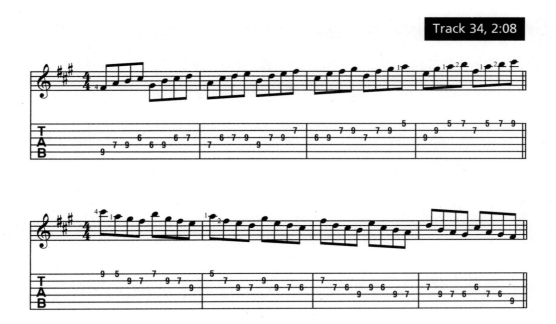

Natural minor scale sequences using pattern #5

The following figure shows ascending and descending sequences that are in the key of F minor in 3rd position. These sequences have no out-of-position notes and offer no opportunities for alternate fingerings. They play fine just as they are!

So, if you're up to it, try doing something a little different with this exercise: After you play the last note in the ascending version, repeat the second-to-last note (the 4th fret of the 1st string). Doing so fills in the rest at the end of the beat and leaves you poised to play the descending sequence immediately, beginning with the 6th fret on the 1st string. This way, you can run the ascending and descending version back to back.

Track 34, 2:48

Up and Down the Scale: Practicing Melodic Minor Scale Sequences

The melodic minor scale has raised 6th and 7th degrees in the ascending version, and normal, unraised versions of those degrees in the descending version. So the descending melodic minor scale is the same as the natural minor scale (which you can read about in the earlier section "It's Only Natural: Practicing Natural Minor Scale Sequences"). So when you play the descending versions of the following exercises, you'll be playing the notes of the natural minor scale. But you should still follow the sequence pattern established by the ascending melodic minor scale exercise that immediately precedes it.

To best appreciate how the melodic minor scale works in a sequence, make sure you play the ascending and descending sequences back to back, without stopping (except to count the rest in the last bar, if one appears) and without losing the rhythm.

Melodic minor scale sequences using pattern #1

The following figure shows ascending and descending sequences in the key of B minor in 7th position. In the ascending version, you may find it easier to play the 8th and 9th frets of the 4th string using fingers 1 and 2 instead of 2 and 3. This makes the 11th-fret note easier to play, because you no longer have to stretch for it. When you move the 1st finger up, you technically change positions (something we try to avoid in this book), but that's okay, because it's only temporary. When you go to the 3rd string, shift back down to 7th position and grab the subsequent out-of-position notes the old-fashioned way: by stretching for them. Many more alternate fingering opportunities exist here, but we just wanted to get you started with an example.

Track 35, 0:00

Melodic minor scale sequences using pattern #2

Try practicing the ascending and descending sequences in the following figure. They're in A minor in 2nd position. These are good sequences to use for bridging the gap between scales and sequences, because they feature six-note stepwise motion in one direction before changing — very scale-like behavior for sequences! Instead of accenting the first note of each triplet group, try accenting the first note of every other set of triplets (once every six notes) to extend the flowing feel.

Track 35, 0:49

Melodic minor scale sequences using pattern #3

The following ascending and descending sequences are in C minor in 3rd position. These are two more sequences that are very scale-like. Plus they're good for conveying drive and purpose because the notes surge forth in one direction for eight notes in a row — an entire octave's worth. So, if you want to be a rebel, play them with a little bit of an edge! The eight-note run really lets you hear the effect of the ascending melodic minor scale, but it's also more interesting than just a straight reading of a scale because of the shifts in direction a sequence brings to the table.

Track 35, 1:41

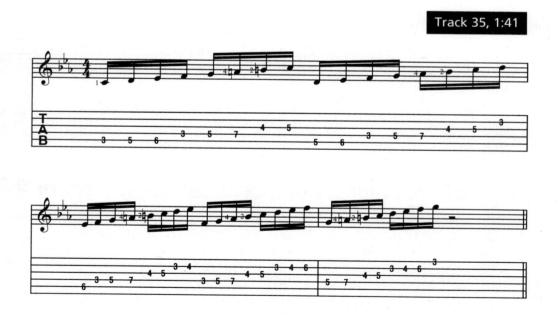

Melodic minor scale sequences using pattern #4

Try playing the following ascending and descending sequences, which are in the key of G minor in 7th position.

Watch out for the out-of-position finger stretch that comes at the end of bar 2. You have to go from your 4th finger to your stretched 1st finger two times, so make sure you hold the stretch long enough for the four successively played notes to sound clearly.

Track 35, 2:17

Melodic minor scale sequences using pattern #5

The following figure shows ascending and descending sequences that are in E minor in 2nd position. Unlike the two previous sequences, which travel long distances in one direction before changing, this one frequently changes directions, providing a bit of sequence mischief. You have to keep your eyes glued to the page while learning this one, as you try to keep your brain nimble enough to negotiate the zigs and zags.

Try out our two alternate approaches for fun on the ascending version. Here's the first one: At bar 2, form a mini-barre with your 1st finger to play the last two notes (which occur on the 2nd and 3rd strings), and then leave the barre in place for the rest of the exercise. Here's the other alternate approach: Play the sixth note of bar 3 (the 4th fret of the 3rd string) using the 2nd finger. This fingering makes the passage more *legato* (sustained), and it also saves you from having to jump your 3rd finger over from the 2nd string — an awkward move that's best avoided.

Track 35, 2:45

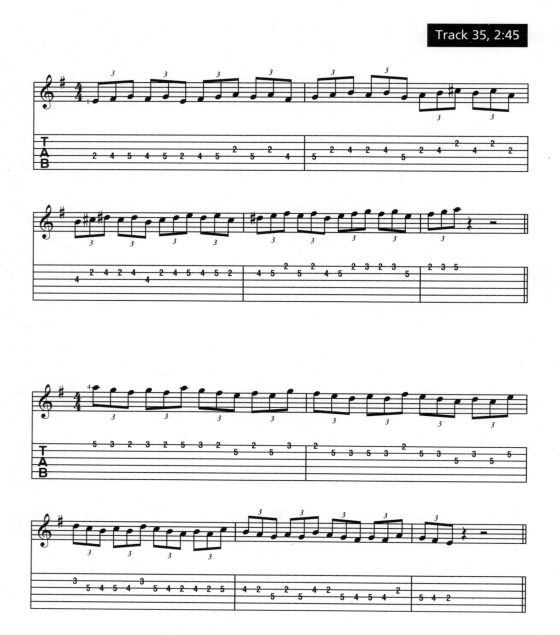

Discovering a More Intense Sound with Harmonic Minor Scale Sequences

In Chapter 5, you discover that the harmonic minor scale is different from the natural minor scale in that it has a raised 7th degree. This gives the scale a "sharper" and "harmonically stronger" sound when compared to the natural minor scale. The scale is often used to evoke a Middle Eastern quality in music. Scale sequences based on the harmonic minor scale are no more difficult than ones based on the natural minor scale, and you may find them easier than melodic minor scale sequences.

As you go through the scale sequences in this section, be sure to play them from low to high slowly, loudly, and deliberately at first to build strength and confidence in your fingers. Then play them faster and lighter to better simulate how the scale sequences will appear in actual pieces. However, no matter how you play them, be sure to maintain your starting tempo and dynamic level (loudness) throughout each sequence.

Harmonic minor scale sequences using pattern #1

The following figure shows ascending and descending sequences in B minor in 7th position. We start you off with a sequence that's really more of an arpeggio than a scale, but it's a good exercise to get your brain thinking in intervals larger than a step.

If you find this pattern a little difficult to grasp at first, look at it again with the idea that it's a three-note grouping placed over a four-note rhythmic scheme. You're more likely to see a figure like this set in triplets, because in eighth notes, the three-note groups don't quite line up neatly with the beats. But that's why we thought it was good to include here: It makes you think. And it sounds unusual.

As a consolation, feel free to employ whatever alternate fingerings you can find. And a lot of them are available here. The key is to look for any two adjacent strings played at the same fret. To get you started, here's a scheme that works well for bar 1 of the ascending version: Play the fourth note (the 9th fret on the 6th string) with the 2nd finger. Play the next 6th-string note (at the 10th fret) with the 3rd finger. If you want another alternate fingering no-brainer, check this one out: Play the last note of bar 2 of the ascending version (5th string, 10th fret) with your 3rd finger. Doing so prevents you from having to jump your 4th finger over, and it keeps the notes sounding smooth and unbroken.

Track 36, 0:00

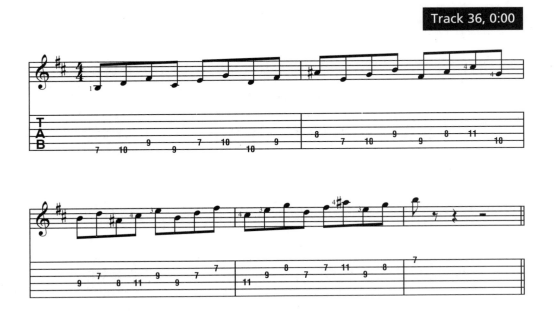

Harmonic minor scale sequences using pattern #2

In the following figure are ascending and descending sequences in the key of C♯ minor in 6th position. A wide stretch occurs between the ninth note (4th string, 6th fret) and the tenth note (4th string, 10th fret) of the ascending version, so it's helpful to open up your whole hand on this one. Also, try rotating your wrist slightly (so that your 4th finger comes toward your body). Doing so helps you play these two distantly separated notes. After tackling those notes, the stretch fest continues, and you must immediately stretch down (toward the nut) to play your 2nd finger on the 7th fret. If this passage gives you trouble, try isolating the eight-note passage that occurs at the second half of bar 1. Play it several times through, working that stretch all the while, until you feel comfortable with it.

Track 36, 0:40

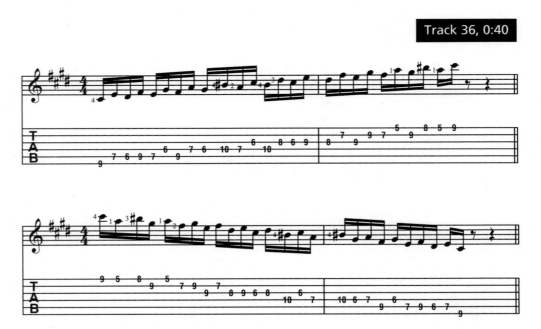

Harmonic minor scale sequences using pattern #3

The following figure shows ascending and descending sequences in E minor in 7th position. Remember that the harmonic minor scale is just like the natural minor scale except for one note — the raised 7th degree, which occurs at the top of the scale. A quick scan of this exercise in E minor music shows that the altered note — D♯ — appears toward the end of bar 2.

As you may have noticed, this sequence takes its sweet time getting to the note that distinguishes it from its more mundane (okay, "natural") sibling. The late appearance of the D♯ means that for the first 21 notes your ear won't know whether you're in E natural minor or E harmonic minor. It also means that you can use a good part of this sequence to satisfy situations calling for E harmonic minor or E natural minor (a folk song melody or another setting where the sharp flavor of a harmonic sequence might be too "spicy").

Track 36, 1:08

Harmonic minor scale sequences using pattern #4

The following figure shows ascending and descending sequences in the key of F♯ minor in 6th position.

As Monty Python would say: And now for something completely different. A common variation of the harmonic minor scale is to start and end on the 5th degree — C♯, in the key of F♯ minor, for example. You preserve the pitches of the original harmonic minor scale, but you change the *tonic,* or starting note. You have an opportunity to hear this *mode* (a segment of a scale that starts and ends on a note other than the tonic) if you start the ascending version of this sequence at bar 5 and play to the end.

This mode, or scale variant, is known by various names, one of which is the impressive-sounding "Phrygian-Dominant." It produces an alternative scale that fits Middle Eastern–sounding songs such as "Hava Nagila" and Duke Ellington's "Caravan."

Track 36, 1:56

Harmonic minor scale sequences using pattern #5

This figure shows ascending and descending sequences in the key of A minor in 7th position. The sequence proceeds conventionally in the ascending version, at least with respect to fingering. Then in bar 2 you see the same fret numbers appearing across two strings, which is a telltale sign of potential mini-barre and alternate-fingering opportunities. Which do you employ?

Here's a secret: It's easier to use a mini-barre when ascending than it is when descending. And in this case, both same-fret moves occur in an upward direction — first at the 9th fret (notes 1 and 2 of bar 2) across strings 3 and 2, and then at the 10th fret (notes 5 and 6). So simply play a 3rd-finger mini-barre at fret 9 and keep it there while you play the first four notes of bar 2. Then slap your 4th-finger barre down immediately above your 3rd-finger barre to play both 10th-fret notes. You don't even have to move your 3rd-finger mini-barre out of the way! It may feel lazy and sloppy — slapping down these mini-barres all over the place — but it works perfectly fine and it's finger legal. Just make sure you're getting a clean, clear tone from those barred notes.

Track 36, 2:59

Practicing Some Pieces Using Minor Scale Sequences

The three pieces in the following sections feature melodies that are based on minor scale sequences for the three different minor scales: natural minor, melodic minor, and harmonic minor. The sequences that you encounter here vary in length, from two-bar phrases to four-bar phrases, and sometimes they contain a slight rhythmic or melodic variation.

In actual music, sequences sometimes aren't observed strictly to the letter. Instead, they're altered according to the context or the taste of the composer. So even if you think you recognize a sequence coming, don't turn on automatic pilot, because the composer may bail on the sequence at any moment and do something unpredictable. And then you may get caught playing a wrong note because you weren't expecting the composer's whim.

"To Work upon the Railroad"

The song "To Work upon the Railroad" is also known by its Gaelic title, "Filimiooriooriay." But we couldn't pronounce that title, let alone tell you what it means. So we named our version according to a lyric that repeats in the song.

"To Work upon the Railroad" is a driving song that features neat two-bar sequences. Compare the first two bars in the music to the next two to see that the melody is nearly the same. The only difference is that you start from a different note.

Also notice the time signature of 6/8, which is felt in 2 (two beats per measure). The time signature 6/8 is often used to give music a light, buoyant feel, so it's a good meter for jigs and marches.

Play this song using natural minor scale pattern #2 in 7th position, starting with the 1st finger. Other than the initial *finger-hop* (playing two consecutive strings at the same fret with the same finger) you must perform in bar 1, this song is fairly easy to play. The second half of the tune is very close to the first half. The difference is that it has slight rhythmic variations.

Track 37

Bach's "Bourrée in E Minor"

The "Bourée in E Minor," which is shown here, is perhaps one of the most famous classical guitar pieces ever written. This piece, which was composed originally for the lute (the guitar's elder cousin) by J. S. Bach, is a two-voice, *contrapuntal* (containing independently moving parts) piece that's written to be performed solo. However, we've arranged it here for one guitar, with the lower line given to the accompanying guitar on the CD. The rhythmic scheme features alternating eighth notes and quarter notes that show off the melodic minor scale nicely in bar 3. Note how the song's opening theme repeats beginning at bar 5, beat 4.

Play this song using melodic minor scale pattern #4 in 4th position, starting with the 2nd finger. Notice that the third note goes out of position, which requires you to play that note (1st-string G) with your 1st finger. After you're back on the 2nd string, the song remains comfortably in 4th position until the second half of the song, when you have to reach down (toward the nut) once again to play the 1st string in bar 6.

This piece of music is so popular that it has been covered by rock band Jethro Tull (who did a swing version of it) and Swedish speed-metal virtuoso Yngwie Malmsteen. Fingerpicker extraordinaire Leo Kottke even did a version of it on a steel-string acoustic guitar.

By the way, a *bourrée* is a type of dance. Composers of Bach's day wrote a lot of suites that were a collection of different dances. Most people don't know the steps to these dances, but we still play the music that was used to accompany them. Maybe that will happen someday to the Chicken Dance. We can only hope.

`Track 38`

"The Full Little Jug"

Here we have another renamed Gaelic song, whose original title, "The Cruiskeen Lawn," roughly translates to "The Full Little Jug." The sequences shown in the music span four bars, so they take longer to repeat than those in "To Work upon the Railroad," which we introduce you to earlier in the chapter. Note that the repeated sequences have slight variations in their rhythm; in other words, they aren't exact rhythmic clones of their predecessors.

"The Full Little Jug" is in the key of B minor and in 6/8 time. The minor key and 6/8 meter may make you think that this tune is similar to "Work upon the Railroad." However, don't be fooled. The melody for "The Full Little Jug" has a more lyrical, less driving feel. Instead, you have more of a scalar approach to the melody (as opposed to the repeated notes found in "To Work upon the Railroad"), except at the end where you have to play wide octave skips. Play this song using harmonic minor scale pattern #3 in 2nd position.

Track 39

Part III
Arpeggios and Arpeggio Sequences

The 5th Wave   By Rich Tennant

"First you play a G7 diminished, followed by an augmented 9th, then a perverted 32nd chord ending with a mangled 11th with a recovering 3rd."

In this part . . .

Playing arpeggios enables you to have a foot in two camps: the single note camp (associated with melody and lead playing) and the chord camp (for rhythm guitar and accompaniment). Technically, you play single notes in the same way you do in Part II for scales and scale sequences, but now you use those single notes to outline chords. Think of playing arpeggios as the transition between playing single notes and thinking — and hearing — chords. Chapter 7 deals with playing major arpeggios (arpeggios based on major chords), and Chapter 8 puts those major arpeggios into sequences. Chapters 9 and 10 do the same thing with minor arpeggios, and Chapters 11 and 12 add seventh chords to your arpeggio arsenal.

Chapter 7

Breaking Out with Major Arpeggios

In This Chapter

▶ Taking on major arpeggios using five patterns

▶ Adding some major arpeggio pieces to your repertoire

An *arpeggio* is a chord whose notes are played one at a time instead of simultaneously. It's sort of the exploded view of a chord (kind of like the pictures you see in the owner's manual to a piece of build-it-yourself furniture). It won't surprise you that in Italian, the word *arpeggio* means "broken chord." You use an arpeggio when some sort of chord is needed but you don't want to plop the notes down all at once. Life would be pretty boring if all you could do with a chord is play all the notes all the time. So this is where arpeggios step in. They're used as accompaniment, as improvisation devices, and as ways to break up scalar playing. (By *scalar,* we mean notes proceeding by steps, or consecutive letter names, with no skips in between.) Arpeggios are also great for getting from point A to point B faster than a scale would take you. Playing arpeggios is like taking giant steps in music.

Throughout this chapter (and this book), we present each arpeggio both in a neck diagram and in music and tab. You can use either figure as a reference, but sometimes it's quicker to use one or the other. For instance, because arpeggios are often related to chord forms, you may find it easier to look at the neck diagrams at first.

After you memorize an arpeggio's fingering pattern, simply move it up or down the neck to a different starting note to produce other major arpeggios. When you do this, the sound of the major chord stays the same. However, as you switch positions, the *key,* or letter name, of the arpeggio changes. To find the correct starting note for each of the 12 major arpeggios, refer to the Cheat Sheet.

Preparing Yourself for Major Chords by Practicing Major Arpeggios

Playing major arpeggios prepares you for music with major chords — and, of course, for music that employs major arpeggios. With arpeggios you think in chords, but you play the notes separately. Bass players have to think in terms of chords and their individual notes. This exercise is good for guitarists, too, because you can play individual notes on the guitar (a melody thing) but use the chords of the song to tell you what notes to play (a chord and accompaniment thing).

As you go through the arpeggios in this section, be sure to play them from low to high slowly, loudly, and deliberately at first to ensure you can play the notes cleanly. Then play them faster and lighter to produce the sound of arpeggios as they appear in real music. However, no matter how you play them, be sure to maintain your starting tempo and dynamic level (loudness) throughout each arpeggio.

Major arpeggio pattern #1

The following figure shows an A major arpeggio in 5th position in both a neck diagram and in music and tab format. Notice that the first note in the music staff has a fingering indication (the small *1* to the left of the note head). This tells you to use the 1st finger of your left hand to play that note.

Major arpeggio pattern #1 includes two *out-of-position notes* (notes that don't fall within the four-fret span defined by the position and that require stretches by the 1st or 4th finger to play). They occur on the 6th and 1st strings. To play these notes, stretch your 4th finger up (toward the bridge) to play the note that occurs one fret higher than the one you would normally play.

Stretching between your 1st and 4th finger is a good physical exercise because it includes (and therefore expands) the in-between fingers. To help loosen your left hand, try playing just the first two notes of the arpeggio back and forth eight times slowly before you play the entire pattern.

Practice this pattern as many times as you need to in order to feel comfortable playing it.

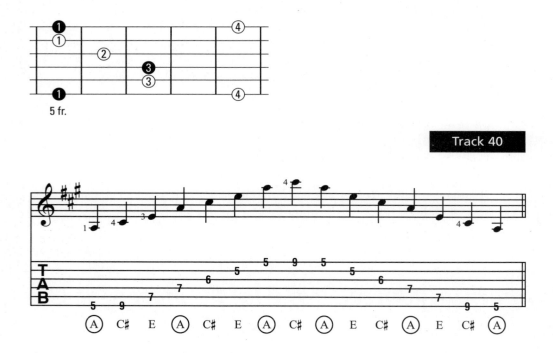

The following figure provides an exercise in rhythm using major arpeggio pattern #1. This pattern is in the key of F major in 1st position in ascending and descending eighth notes. Because it doesn't take many notes to complete the pattern, we take you through it twice. The pattern in this figure occurs in the lowest position, where the frets are widest, so you can use it as a good stretching exercise.

Major arpeggio pattern #2

Major arpeggio pattern #2 starts with the 4th finger on the 6th string and includes no out-of-position notes. So you can enjoy a stretch-free series of exercises for a while! And because you don't have to worry about stretching, you can focus on developing another skill.

For example, as an option, flatten out your 1st finger to play the consecutive notes on the 4th, 3rd, and 2nd strings, all of which occur at the same fret (the 5th, in this case). Think of this flattened 1st finger as a *mini-barre* (a partial barre that covers just two or three strings). This technique is especially helpful when you want to create a more *legato* (smooth and connected) sound between the notes.

The following figure shows the neck diagram as well as the corresponding music and tab for major arpeggio pattern #2 in the key of C major. Practice this pattern so you can play it eight times in a row perfectly, including any mini-barre alternate fingerings (should you choose to employ them).

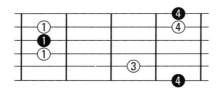

5 fr.

Track 41

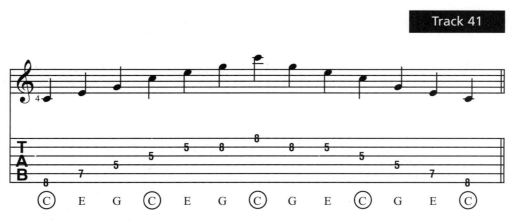

After you're comfortable with the pattern, try major arpeggio pattern #2 in 7th-position D major. For a legato sound, use a 4th-finger mini-barre at the 10th fret for the top two strings.

Major arpeggio pattern #3

Major arpeggio patterns #1 and #2 have a range of two or more octaves, but major arpeggio patterns #3, #4, and #5 span a bit less than two octaves. The narrower octave ranges mean that you don't have as many available notes to play, making the exercises shorter. But, luckily that also means the patterns become easier to learn and memorize.

Major arpeggio pattern #3 begins on the 5th string (not the 6th, as in the previous two patterns). The pattern starts with the 1st finger and includes an out-of-position note on the 5th string. You must stretch up (toward the bridge) with your 4th finger to reach the out-of-position note, because it occurs one fret above (higher on the neck) where the finger naturally falls.

The following figure provides the neck diagram and corresponding music and tab for major arpeggio pattern #3 in the key of D major. Practice this pattern as many times as you need to in order to get the stretch feeling comfortable and sounding smooth.

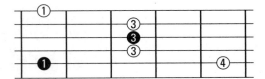

5 fr.

Track 42

Pattern #3 provides an opportunity for using alternate fingerings to make the arpeggios a little easier to play, especially in legato passages. Try forming a mini-barre with your 3rd finger to play any combination of notes that falls consecutively on the 4th, 3rd, and 2nd strings.

To create a legato sound in the following exercise, which is in 8th-position F major, try using a 3rd-finger mini-barre at the 10th fret for the 4th, 3rd, and 2nd strings. Doing so will help these speedy sixteenth notes flow a little easier.

Major arpeggio pattern #4

The next figure shows major arpeggio pattern #4 in the key of F major in both a neck diagram and in music and tab format. Practice this pattern slowly, without worrying about the rhythm. Do this until you can play all the notes equally well. Then try the exercise in rhythm.

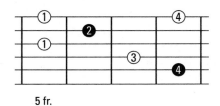

Track 43

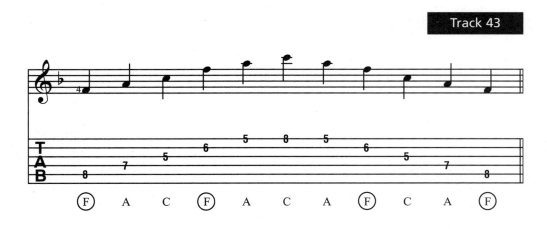

The following exercise is in 3rd-position E♭ major. Because the first five notes of the pattern can be held down as a chord, try this exercise both *staccato* (playing each note with the fingertip and lifting the finger off the string immediately) and legato (holding down the left hand as a chord and letting the notes ring out whenever possible).

Major arpeggio pattern #5

Major arpeggio pattern #5 is a four-string pattern whose lowest note is on the 4th string. It starts with the 1st finger and includes an out-of-position note on the 4th string. You must stretch your 4th finger up (toward the bridge) to reach this note, because it occurs one fret above (higher on the neck) where the finger naturally falls.

Note that in addition to including the starting finger next to the first note in the music, we also include the fingering for the out-of-position note (in this case, a *4*). To get you safely back into the pattern, we also provide, as a reminder, the next fingering indication (in this case, a *3*), which is what you would normally play.

The following figure shows the neck diagram and corresponding music and tab for major arpeggio pattern #5 in the key of G major. In order to make a smooth move from the 4th string to the 3rd string, practice this pattern several times before proceeding to the rhythm exercise.

5 fr.

Track 44

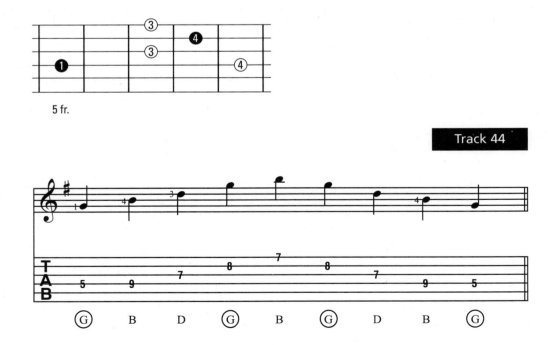

Consider the reasons for using an alternate fingering in this next exercise, which is in 3rd-position F major. As a pair, the 2nd and 3rd fingers are stronger than the 3rd and 4th ones. So for the top three strings, instead of using the fingers indicated in the pattern (3-4-3), use 2-3-2.

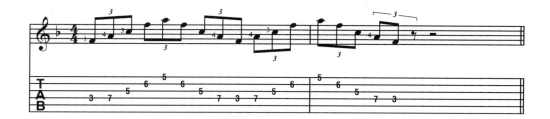

Applying Your Skills: Performing Pieces Using Major Arpeggios

It's unusual to find music that's made up of just major arpeggios. However, if you're determined, there's one genre you can look to: military bugle. The bugle can play the notes of a major chord easily, but it has a much more difficult time playing any other notes. If you hum or whistle some common bugle calls that you know, such as "Reveille" and "Taps," you're sounding the notes of a major arpeggio. Instead of the aforementioned titles, though, we've chosen two lesser known bugle calls that are quite inventive in their melodies — despite their use of only the notes of the major chord.

"To the Colors"

"To the Colors," which is shown in the following figure, is a piece that's played to honor the nation, as in a salute to the "colors," or flag. This tune is given the same respect in a military setting as the national anthem. For our arrangement of this piece, you use major arpeggio patterns #1 and #2.

This piece contains a dotted eighth note followed by a sixteenth note, which gives the music a kind of buoyant feel. The comma at bar 9 tells you to take a slight pause before continuing. You can play the 5th-fret notes using a mini-barre (by flattening your 1st finger), but be sure not to make the notes too legato. (You can read more about creating a mini-barre earlier in the chapter.) Keeping a slightly detached feel between the notes helps to better emulate the sound of a bugle, which is the effect you're going for.

Track 45

Moderately

Major arpeggio pattern #2

Major arpeggio pattern #2

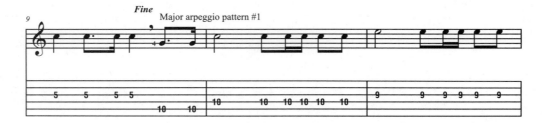

Fine Major arpeggio pattern #1

D.C. al Fine

"Retreat"

"Retreat," in this case, doesn't mean "let's get the heck out of here." Instead, it's used to signal the end of the official day. As you can imagine, this tune's mood is mellower than the rousing "Reveille" and a bit more informal than the stately "To the Colors." Refer to the following figure to see the music for this tune.

To play our arrangement of "Retreat," use major arpeggio patterns #3 and #4, and note that the position shift is on a common note (C) between bars 10 and 11. Try to finesse this shift so the listener isn't aware that you're changing positions and fingers. Doing so helps you develop legato playing over a position shift.

Track 46

Chapter 8

Discovering How to Play Major Arpeggio Sequences

In This Chapter

▶ Practicing major arpeggio sequences using five patterns

▶ Performing pieces with major arpeggio sequences

*I*n some ways, playing an arpeggio sequence can be easier than playing a plain old arpeggio. Because major arpeggios have only the notes of a major chord, you have to cover great distances in a relatively short amount of time, rhythmically speaking. On the other hand, an arpeggio sequence often gives you a little more time to go back and forth among the chord tones instead of just vaulting up and down the pattern.

In this chapter, we show you how to play sequences composed of the notes of major chord arpeggios. You can develop the skill to change directions on a dime as well as skip up and down the neck in wide intervals, all while using the notes of the major chord as your palette. At the end of the chapter, you get to rock out with two classic rock 'n' roll grooves.

Just as you do in your arpeggio work, you should move all the sequences presented in this chapter up and down the neck to produce other major arpeggio sequences. This ensures that you can find major arpeggio sequences to match any chord. If you need a little refresher on the names of the starting notes for your arpeggio sequences, refer to the neck diagram on the Cheat Sheet. It lists the pitches of the frets on all six strings.

Picking Up On Major Arpeggio Sequences

Even though you may find it easier to play sequences than arpeggios in general, you still have to be prepared to perform some of the challenging techniques that present themselves in all arpeggio playing. Some of these challenging techniques include switching strings with consecutive notes at the same fret and fingering *out-of-position notes* (notes that don't fall directly under the fingers and that you have to reach for).

In this chapter, the out-of-position notes are labeled in the standard music notation staff according to the rules of the pattern, but you're welcome to find your own substitutions. Just don't get yourself out of position for too long if you decide to play with alternate fingerings, because you may accidentally play a wrong note.

Major arpeggio sequences using pattern #1

The following figure shows ascending and descending sequences with wide skips between each pair of notes. Each note is on a different string. Sometimes you even have to skip over a string to play the next note. If you play both with a pick and with your right-hand fingers, try this one using a fingerstyle approach so you can concentrate on your left hand.

Before trying these exercises in their entirety, try playing just the two sets of notes that occur on the 6th and 1st strings as a stretching warm-up. That is, on the 6th string, go back and forth several times between the 6th and 10th frets with your 1st and 4th fingers; then do the same thing on the 1st string. This stretching will help you hit the out-of-position notes with less strain and more accuracy.

Track 47, 0:00

Now try playing the following ascending and descending sequences, which are in the key of D in 10th position. Some of the skips here require you to jump over two strings, so if you're a flatpicker, definitely go to a right-hand fingerstyle approach for this one (or at least until you master the left-hand fingerings).

For finger-strengthening purposes, you should play these exercises, as you should all the arpeggios in this book, with the string-hopping approach. This is where the fingertips play one note at a time and the notes don't sustain. But if you want to have a more *legato* sound, where the notes ring through, you can achieve that easily by using held-down chord forms and/or barres.

For example, try holding down a 1st-finger barre at the 10th fret to play the following sequences. Then place your 3rd and 2nd fingers down on the 5th and 3rd strings. If you do this, you find you have to move only one finger — the 4th — so that it can grab those 14th-fret notes on the 1st and 6th strings and the 12th-fret notes on the 4th string.

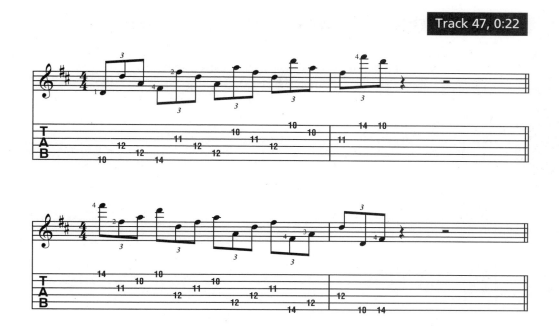

Major arpeggio sequences using pattern #2

Major arpeggio pattern #2 includes three notes in a row that occur at the same fret on consecutive strings. You may find it easier to play these notes with your 1st finger flattened. When you flatten your finger to play just two or three strings, you create a *mini-barre*.

The following figure shows four-note ascending and descending sequences in the key of B in 4th position. If you want the notes in this exercise to ring through, try this alternate approach: Barre the 2nd, 3rd, and 4th strings with your 1st finger, and then place your 4th finger on the 6th string and your 3rd finger on the 5th string. In the ascending version, this sets you up to play the first four beats with a completely stationary left hand. At beat four-and-a-half, you have to move your 4th finger from the 6th string to the 2nd to grab that 7th-fret note. The 4th finger can then create a mini-barre in bar 2 to play the last two notes effortlessly.

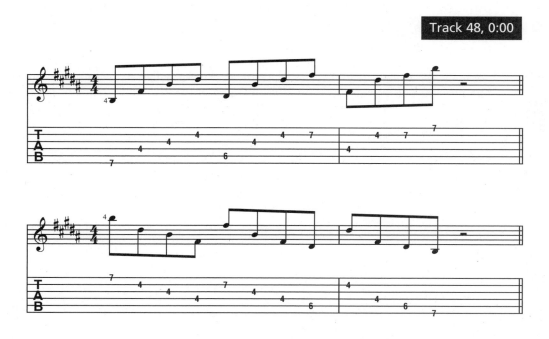

The wide skips in the following ascending and descending sequences (key of E♭, 8th position) mean that every note is played on a different string. (The exceptions to this occur between the last two notes in the ascending version and between notes 3, 4, and 5 in the descending version.) Sometimes you have to skip over a string — or even two — to play the next note.

Flatpickers may want to leave their picks on the music stand (or between their teeth) for this one, because these sequences are a lot easier to play with the individual right-hand fingers.

Track 48, 0:22

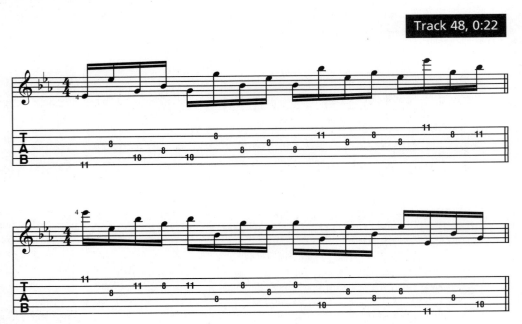

Major arpeggio sequences using pattern #3

The following ascending and descending sequences are in the key of E in 7th position. Because an out-of-position stretch occurs at the beginning of the ascending version, practice playing just the first three notes several times, in a loop, before playing through the entire sequence.

You can play these sequences using the written fingerings, or you can use the following alternate fingerings: In the ascending version, play note 7 with the 2nd finger (not the 3rd) to avoid having to jump your 3rd finger over from the 3rd string. Doing this also sets you up to play the rest of the exercise without having to move the 2nd and 3rd fingers. Instead these fingers become anchors. When it's time to play the 2nd string (in bar 2), use the 4th finger; use the 1st finger (the only one left!) to play the 1st-string notes.

Track 49, 0:00

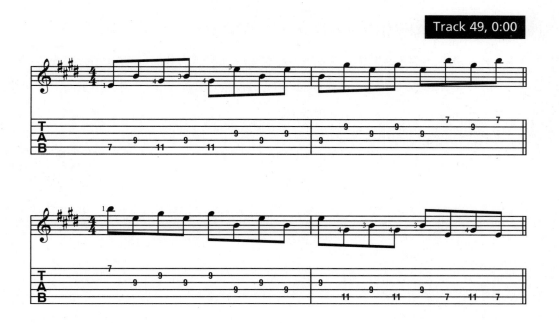

For the next set of ascending and descending sequences (key of D♭, 4th position), you can play the arpeggios with the written fingering, or you can try forming a mini-barre with your 3rd finger to play the 6th-fret notes, which occur on the 4th, 3rd, and 2nd strings. You'll have to move the barre around a bit, though, because it's difficult to play the 1st-string note while holding the barre perfectly stationary. So move it out of the way when you have to, and then put it back as soon as the 1st string has sounded for its full duration.

Track 49, 0:27

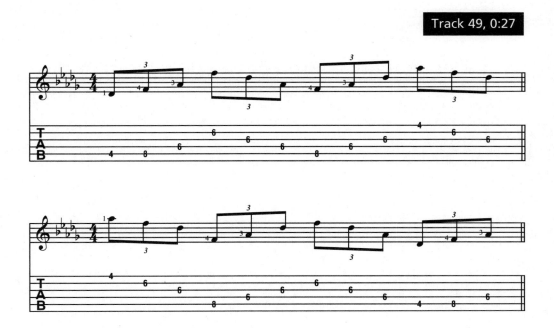

Major arpeggio sequences using pattern #4

You can play the following ascending and descending sequences, which are in the key of A in 9th position, as written, or by using a 1st-finger mini-barre across the top three strings. If you go with the mini-barre, you can then play the ascending version by pre-fretting the 4th, 3rd, and 2nd fingers. That way, for the first ten notes, you don't have to move a left-hand finger at all. In the descending version, the finger movement comes right at the beginning, with a lifting of the 4th finger on the 1st string; but then the rest of the figure is played with stationary fingers.

Track 50, 0:00

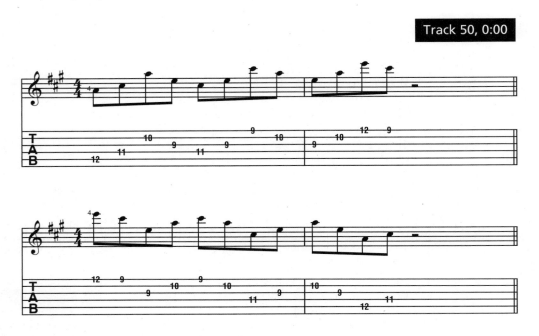

In the following ascending and descending sequences (key of D, 2nd position), you may not have any problem with the stationary left-hand approach that results from employing a held-down chord, but the way the notes fall on the strings may present you with a right-hand challenge, especially if you're playing these exercises with a flatpick.

Don't practice these sequences too slowly, because doing so tends to interfere with the natural swinging movement of the wrist and may affect your accuracy with a pick.

Track 50, 0:20

Major arpeggio sequences using pattern #5

In the following ascending and descending sequences (key of E♭, 1st position), we give the fingering indications according to the rules of the pattern. But truthfully, almost no one uses the 4th finger on the sixth note in the ascending sequence, especially after placing the 4th finger on the 4th string immediately preceding. Instead substitute the 3rd finger there. And for the following note on the 3rd string, use the 2nd finger. You can even hold down all three fingers for a nice legato sound. Remember that we provide fingerings as a *reference,* not as gospel!

Track 51, 0:00

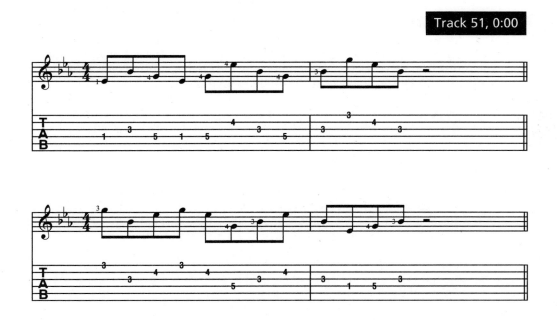

You can play the following ascending and descending sequences (key of A♭, 6th position) with the written fingerings. But if you want to try something different for the ascending version, use the following alternate-fingering scheme: Play the fifth note with the 1st finger (not the 3rd, as indicated). Then for note 8, play the 2nd string with the 2nd finger. And for the eleventh note, play the 1st string with the 1st finger.

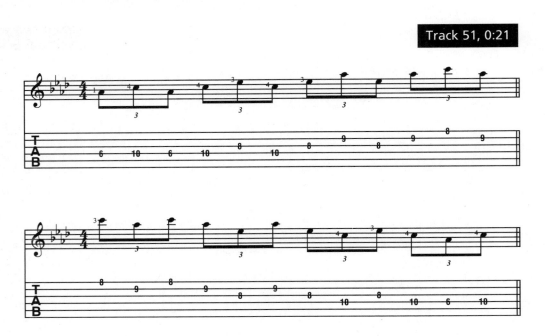

Track 51, 0:21

Playing Pieces That Feature Major Arpeggio Sequences

The two pieces in this section feature prominent guitar parts based on arpeggio sequences. You may notice that we use the phrase "prominent guitar parts" instead of "melody." That's because an arpeggio is somewhere between a melody and a chord — it carries elements of each. These parts sound great by themselves and in front of a band, but they may not seem melodic to you in the traditional sense. However, the arpeggio sequences used here provide a great sound and nice groove, and they're totally at home in a featured, or lead, context.

There's a scene in the movie *Back to the Future* that takes place during the "Enchantment Under the Sea" dance at the high school. The hero, played by Michael J. Fox, takes the stage and with a borrowed guitar leads the band in two numbers, "Johnny B. Goode" and "Earth Angel." We modeled our two tunes on the grooves of those early rock 'n' roll classics. Be sure to turn the flux capacitor on your amp up to 11 when you play these!

"Blues Riff in B"

The form of "Blues Riff in B" is the classic 12-bar blues, but it's played the rock 'n' roll way, which is in a straight-eighth feel (not a shuffle or swing). In the music provided for this piece, you'll notice some nice syncopations in the odd-numbered bars and in bar 10. These syncopations give the progression a slight kick and make it fun to play.

As the title suggests, this song is in the key of B. Note that all five major arpeggio patterns are used in this piece, but not in order. We like to keep things interesting for you by mixing up the order of the patterns! This progression fits many styles of music that are played as a 12-bar blues in a straight-eighth feel, such as songs by Chuck Berry.

Track 52

Medium Blues/Rock

"Doo-Wop Groove in A"

Unlike the syncopated style of "Blues Riff in B," the tune "Doo-Wop Groove in A" (in the key of A, naturally), features a slower, more relaxed feel. This song, which is shown in the following figure, uses patterns 1, 2, 3, and 4. These patterns should be played in a flowing, legato style. You may notice that patterns 1, 2, and 4 correspond to the movable barre chords based on the open chords E, G, and C. Playing the notes of an arpeggio from within a held-down chord allows the notes to ring.

The last bar of "Doo-Wop Groove in A" should be played as a chord form, and the wavy line tells you to separate the notes slightly instead of sounding them simultaneously.

Track 53

Moderately, in 2

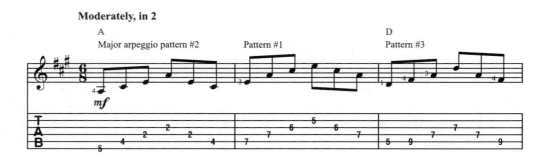

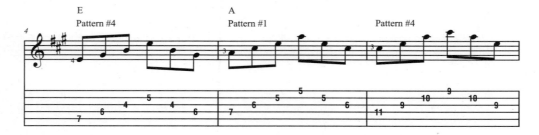

Chapter 9

Getting to Know Minor Arpeggios

· ·

· ·

Minor arpeggios can be applied to music in minor keys and to music in major keys that contain minor chords. So that includes just about everything! When the music you're playing calls for a minor chord, you can of course play a minor chord, but you can sometimes use a minor arpeggio, which provides a different texture. You can also use a minor arpeggio as a single-note idea if the underlying harmony corresponds to the arpeggio's minor chord counterpart. Mastering minor arpeggios gets you thinking and playing in minor terms, both from a harmonic standpoint and a melodic one. Also, playing the straightforward arpeggios contained in this chapter prepares you for the fancy stuff, such as the minor chord arpeggio sequences that you encounter in Chapter 10.

In this chapter, we cover five patterns for playing minor arpeggios. You get to apply these arpeggios in a number of musical settings comprised of different rhythms in various keys. As a bonus, you get to play minor arpeggios over two classically inspired pieces, which appear at the end of the chapter.

Throughout this chapter (and the book), we present arpeggio patterns in both neck diagrams and in music and tab. Use whichever figure you're most comfortable with, but remember that sometimes it's quicker to use one or the other, depending on the circumstance. For example, because arpeggios are often related to chord forms, you may find it easier to look at the neck diagrams first — especially if you're used to reading chord diagrams.

Practice the arpeggio exercises in this chapter as many times as necessary to make the notes flow smoothly. And be sure that you can play the exercises at a steady tempo. After you memorize and master an arpeggio pattern's fingering, simply move it up or down the neck to a different starting note to produce other minor arpeggios. The sound of the minor chord stays the same. However, as you switch positions, the key, or letter name, of the arpeggio changes. If you need a little help finding the names of different starting notes on the strings, refer to the Cheat Sheet.

Working On Minor Arpeggios

A minor arpeggio is a very close cousin to a major arpeggio, at least in terms of its DNA. In fact, one note defines the difference between a major and a minor arpeggio — and that's the 3rd of the chord. So if you came to this chapter by way of Chapter 7 (major arpeggios), the exercises here may appear eerily familiar, because the majority of the notes in any minor arpeggio and its corresponding major counterpart are the same! But the musical effect couldn't be more different. So if you want cheerful arpeggios, go back two chapters. But if you're ready for minor-key gloom, read on!

As you work through the arpeggios in this section, play each one slowly, loudly, and deliberately at first to build strength and confidence in your fingers. Then play them faster and lighter, which better simulates the way arpeggios appear in real music. Just be sure to maintain your starting tempo and dynamic level (loudness) throughout each exercise.

Minor arpeggio pattern #1

The following figure shows an A minor arpeggio in 5th position in both a neck diagram and in music and tab format. Notice that the first note of the exercise (here and in the rest of this chapter) has a fingering indication in the music staff (the small *1* to the left of the A notehead). This indicator tells you to use the 1st finger of your left hand to play that note.

Because minor arpeggio pattern #1 includes no *out-of-position notes* (notes that don't fall within the four-fret span defined by the position and that require stretches by the 1st or 4th finger to play), this pattern is great for becoming familiar with the sound of a minor arpeggio without having to worry about stretching. You can sometimes employ the technique of flattening a finger into a *mini-barre* (a partial barre that covers just two or three strings) to play consecutive strings at the same fret. You may find this easier than jumping the finger from string to string, especially at fast tempos.

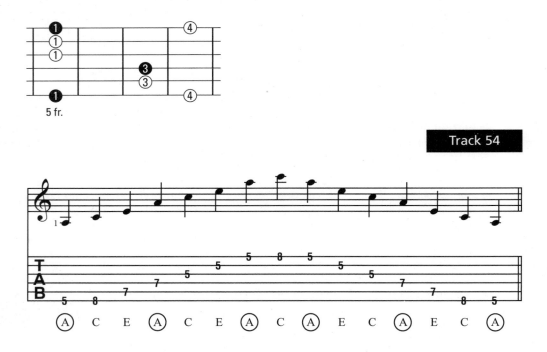

The following figure shows minor arpeggio pattern #1 in the key of F minor in 1st position. An arpeggio has fewer notes than a scale, so the arpeggio may seem a little short. To make sure you get your money's worth, we take you up and down the pattern twice. Make sure to closely monitor your rhythm here; the tendency is to rush on the way up and drag on the way down. Break out the metronome to help keep your practice honest!

Now try this exercise, which is in 8th-position C minor. If you want to achieve a more *legato* (smooth and connected) sound, you can employ two mini-barres, each with a different finger. For example, play a 3rd-finger mini-barre for the notes on the 4th and 5th strings. Then play a 1st-string mini-barre on the 3rd, 2nd, and 1st strings.

Minor arpeggio pattern #2

Check out the following figure, which shows a C minor arpeggio in 5th position in a neck diagram and in music and tab. Of the seven notes in this pattern, the 4th finger plays four of them, so use this exercise to concentrate on building up your 4th-finger strength. Make sure you keep your finger curved and don't let the knuckles flatten out.

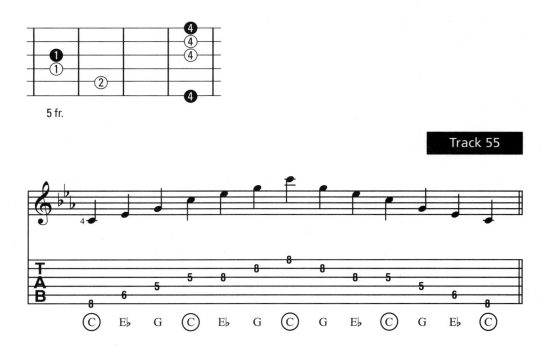

The following figure shows minor arpeggio pattern #2 in 2nd-position A minor. For a more legato effect, try a 4th-finger mini-barre across the top three strings. If you have a little more trouble playing a 4th-finger mini-barre than playing a 1st- or 2nd-finger mini-barre, it may help to stack the 3rd finger on top of the 4th and bear down with both fingers.

In the following figure is minor arpeggio pattern #2 in 3rd-position B♭ minor. *Pre-fret* (that is, place your fingers down before you start to play the exercise) the 6th and 5th strings with your 4th and 2nd fingers. Pre-fretting is almost like getting a head start on playing the exercise. Look for other opportunities to get your fingers in position before the exercise begins.

Minor arpeggio pattern #3

The previous two patterns have a range of at least two octaves. Minor arpeggio patterns #3, #4, and #5 span a bit less than two octaves. So there are fewer notes here in this pattern. The good news is that you may find you can memorize these patterns a little faster.

To see the neck diagram and corresponding music and tab for minor arpeggio pattern #3 in the key of D minor, check out the following figure. Play through the notes of the figure slowly to make sure you can get all the notes to sound smooth and clear. Then gradually build up speed in order to prepare for the exercises in rhythm that follow.

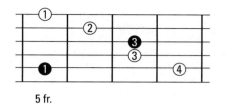

5 fr.

Track 56

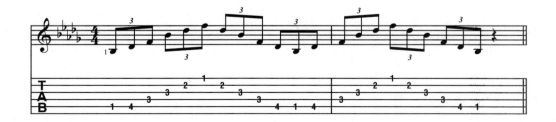

Check out this figure, which shows minor arpeggio pattern #3 in 3rd-position C minor. This sequence presents a good opportunity to try a 3rd-finger mini-barre across the 4th and 3rd strings. Doing so helps create a legato sound.

The next exercise you can try is in 1st-position B♭ minor, and you can take a *staccato* approach here, where all the notes are short and detached. Use no mini-barres, and jump the 3rd finger across the 4th and 3rd strings as the normal fingering for the pattern indicates.

Minor arpeggio pattern #4

The following figure shows minor arpeggio pattern #4 in the key of F minor in both a neck diagram and in music and tab format. Play the notes slowly at first so you can get familiar with the new pattern. Then work to get the notes smooth and up to tempo before going on to the exercises in rhythm that follow.

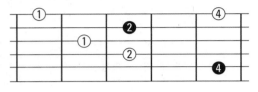

4 fr.

Track 57

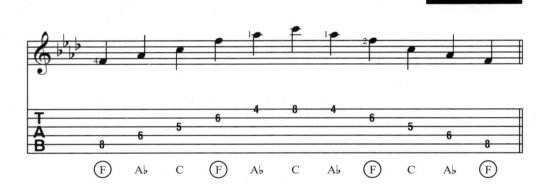

Now try the following pattern #4 exercise, which is in 3rd-postion E♭ minor. The standard way to play this pattern is to use the 2nd finger on the 2nd string. Doing so keeps you in position. However, you do have to stretch down (toward the nut) to reach the first 1st-string note. You can eliminate the stretch between the 2nd and 1st strings if you substitute the 3rd finger for the 2nd finger on the 2nd string.

The following figure shows minor arpeggio pattern #4 in 2nd-position D minor. Because you're in a low position to begin with and have to stretch down to the 1st fret, you're stretching the maximum possible distance between both your 2nd and 1st fingers and your 1st and 4th fingers. So remember this exercise when you feel like you need to limber up your left hand.

Minor arpeggio pattern #5

Refer to the following figure, which shows the neck diagram and corresponding music and tab for minor arpeggio pattern #5 in the key of G minor. Play the pattern slowly at first to get your fingers used to playing the notes that fall on the different strings and frets. Then gradually speed up to prepare for the rhythmic exercises that follow.

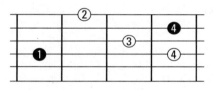

5 fr.

Track 58

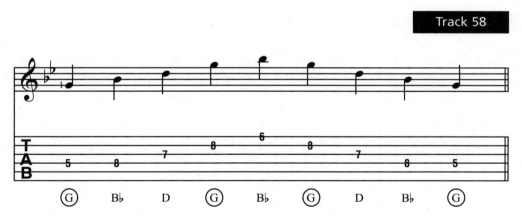

G   B♭   D   G   B♭   G   D   B♭   G

When you feel secure with minor arpeggio pattern #5, give the following exercise in 7th-position A minor a try. If you're game, here's an alternate fingering that works well and avoids using the 4th finger. Starting at the second note of the pattern, use fingers 3-2-3-1 (instead of 4-3-4-2) and play all the notes staccato (short, separated, and detached).

For the next exercise, which is in 3rd-position F minor, play an approach that contrasts with the previous exercise by letting the top four strings ring out as a chord. Here's how to do it: Play the second note with the 3rd finger (instead of the 4th) as you did in the previous exercise. Then use fingers 2-4-1 for the top three strings. Doing so enables you to keep all four fingers down and hold them while they sustain after being played.

Playing Pieces with Minor Arpeggios

Even though there are many more examples of music that use major arpeggios for their principal melodic material, we managed to come up with a couple of pieces that feature minor arpeggios. We found some great pieces in the catalog of Wolfgang Amadeus Mozart, a child star who died when he was only 34. Despite a relatively short life, he proved to be prolific, and, more important, he produced some of the world's most beautiful and enduring music. The following two pieces were inspired by his skill with minor material and arpeggios.

"Wolfgang's Whistle"

"Wolfgang's Whistle" was adapted from a Mozart piano sonata. And even though it was designed for practicing minor arpeggios, it contains major arpeggios, too. Actual pieces of music often mix minor and major, so this is a chance to hear how the two qualities interact. Seeing the reappearance of the major arpeggio is a good thing, because it reinforces what you work on in Chapters 7 and 8. Plus it provides a setting where you can hear how a major sound can benefit not only a major-key piece but a minor-key piece as well.

As you can see in the following music, "Wolfgang's Whistle" uses minor arpeggio patterns #1 through #4. The rests after each five-note ascent allow you to shift positions easily so you can set up for the next pattern. The other instrument heard on the CD answers the ascending arpeggios with a scalar figure, providing a nice contrast of arpeggios and scales.

Track 59

"Amadeus's Air"

Like "Wolfgang's Whistle," "Amadeus's Air" is also taken from a Mozart composition (a piano concerto) and is based on ascending arpeggios (using patterns #1, #2, and #3). But this piece is a little trickier to play because the patterns don't start on the beat. Instead, they start after a sixteenth rest. The accompaniment part *does* hit the downbeat, though, so you can use the CD as a cue to start your pattern. Also, the patterns are longer here than in the previous piece — seven notes instead of five, and they cover all six strings. The good news about this piece is that you get two beats of rest in between each pattern to allow you to set up for the next arpeggio. Two beats should be plenty of time to switch positions effortlessly.

The last bar in "Amadeus's Air," which is shown in the following figure, starts with a note lower than the note you start the pattern from on the 6th string. (Minor arpeggio pattern #3 normally starts on the 5th string.) You can form a mini-barre with your 1st finger for the first two notes in bar 8, which helps make the notes easier to play.

Track 60

Chapter 10

Looking at Minor Arpeggio Sequences

. . . .

In This Chapter

▶ Practicing minor arpeggio sequences using five patterns

▶ Playing pieces using minor arpeggio sequences

. . . .

*B*ecause minor arpeggios have only the notes of a minor chord, you often have to cover great distances in a relatively short amount of musical time — one chord tone per note. However, many sequences have you switching direction to revisit previously played notes. In this chapter, you play arpeggio sequences composed of the notes of the minor arpeggios you practice in Chapter 9 — the notes of the minor chord (the root, 3rd, and 5th).

Practice the patterns in this chapter repeatedly, or until you can play them easily from memory. Then, simply move a pattern up or down the neck to different starting notes to transpose it to different keys. If you're rusty on naming the starting notes of the arpeggio sequences as you move around the neck, refer to the neck diagram on the Cheat Sheet that lists the note names of the frets. Note that in this chapter we present the ascending and descending sequences in pairs.

Adding Minor Arpeggio Sequences to Your Practice Sessions

As with straight arpeggios, arpeggio sequences present challenges that are common to all arpeggio work, including playing the same fret on consecutive strings and stretching to reach out-of-position notes. (An *out-of-position note* is one that doesn't fall within the four-fret span defined by the position and that requires a stretch by the 1st or 4th finger to play it.) In some cases, a sequence can even put you in a "loop" of uncomfortable left-hand fingering. When these types of cases come up, you're welcome to find your own alternate fingerings. Just be sure that you can get back on track with the normal fingering if you (or a teacher) decide to try an alternate fingering for a certain passage.

As you work through the arpeggio sequences in this section, start out by playing each one slowly and assertively. After you memorize a sequence and are comfortable with the fingering, try playing it faster and with a lighter touch. Doing so will better simulate the way the sequence will be played in an actual piece of music.

Minor arpeggio sequences using pattern #1

The following figure shows ascending and descending sequences in the key of B♭ minor in 6th position. These sequences contain no out-of-position notes, and that means you don't have to stretch to reach any of the notes. Most of the challenges in this exercise come from playing large interval skips, which is more difficult than playing in stepwise motion (by consecutive letter names).

You can play this exercise with the indicated fingering, or you can try a simple alternative approach that will yield a more *legato* (sustained and ringing) sound. Play the first four notes with the fingering as indicated by the pattern (1, 3, 4, 3). But instead of jumping your 3rd finger over to play the 8th fret on string 4, as you normally would, use the 2nd finger. Then place a 1st-finger *mini-barre* (a partial barre that covers just two or three strings) across the top three strings. You may have to stretch a little to cover the one-fret gap between your 2nd and 1st fingers, but it shouldn't be too uncomfortable.

Track 61, 0:00

The following figure features ascending and descending sequences in the key of D minor in 10th position. To create a legato feel, barre all six strings with the 1st finger. Then place your 2nd and 3rd fingers on the 5th and 4th strings. This preparation sets you up to play the figure with a minimum amount of left-hand movement — always a sure way to enhance legato playing.

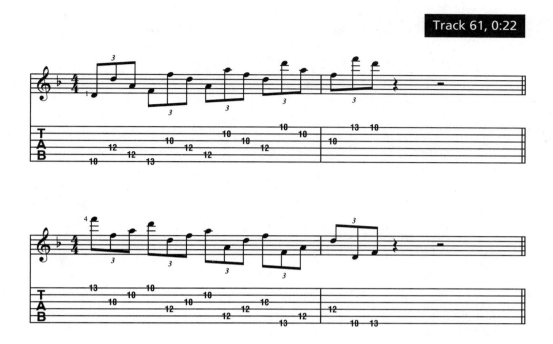

Minor arpeggio sequences using pattern #2

In the following figure are ascending and descending sequences in the key of B minor in 4th position. They're based on minor arpeggio pattern #2, which features three notes in a row that fall at the same fret on consecutive strings. You may sometimes find it easier to play these notes with your 4th finger flattened, creating a mini-barre. Employing a mini-barre will also help you produce a more legato sound.

A legato arpeggio is often a perfect texture to fill out a part that supports a melody playing above it. You can also form a mini-barre with your 1st finger to play the 4th-fret notes on the 4th and 3rd strings, which further enhances the legato sound.

Check out the following figure, which shows ascending and descending sequences in the key of E♭ minor in 8th position. The wide skips here have you jumping strings with your right hand fairly often, sometimes skipping over two strings to reach the next note. So drop your flatpick (if you're using one) and try this one fingerstyle so you can focus on your left hand.

In the ascending version, it may help you to break the two-bar sequence into separate parts for practicing. The first part includes notes 1 through 6, all of which can be played easily without employing a mini-barre or alternate fingerings. Notes 7 through 13 can be played more easily if you form a 1st-string mini-barre across the 4th and 3rd strings to grab those 8th-fret notes. And for the final three notes, flatten your 4th finger into a mini-barre and slap it down at the 11th fret, starting at note 14.

Track 62, 0:20

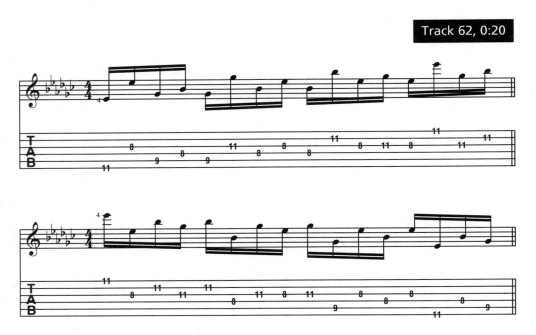

Minor arpeggio sequences using pattern #3

Check out the following figure, which shows ascending and descending sequences in 7th-position E minor.

In the ascending version, you can play the pattern with a legato effect that allows you to sustain the first note of each two-beat group — a handy accompaniment approach — by following this alternate-fingering plan: Play the first five notes normally, holding down the fifth note (and letting it sustain) with your 4th finger. Then play notes 6, 7, and 8 with your 3rd, 2nd, and 3rd fingers. In bar 2, move your 1st finger to the 2nd string to play the two 8th-fret notes. Next move your 1st finger to the 1st string to play the 7th-fret notes, and then move your 2nd finger to the 2nd string to play the next-to-last note. The notes sustain, yet the fingers move during the pattern — producing a feeling of finger independence and a useful accompaniment effect.

Track 63, 0:00

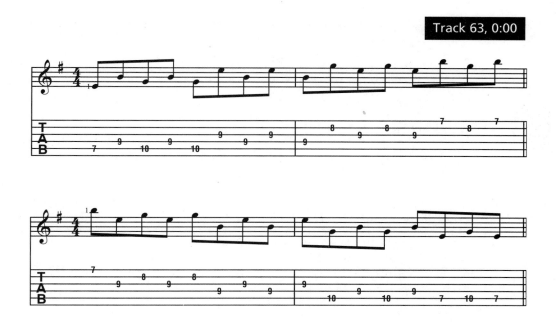

When you're ready to move on, check out the following figure, which shows six-note ascending and descending sequences in 4th-position C♯ minor. The ascending sequence poses an alternate-fingering opportunity where only the 4th finger has to move to play the entire sequence with a legato feel. You play all the frets with the fingering indicated by the pattern except for the 3rd string, which you play with the 4th finger. Try it slowly at first to get used to moving the 4th finger from the 5th string to the 3rd and back. After you're comfortable, gradually speed up.

For the descending version, however, you execute the legato technique a little differently. Here you have to move both the 4th *and* 3rd fingers. Play the first four notes using fingers 1, 2, 3, and 4. For the fifth note, move the 3rd finger over from the 3rd string to the 4th to play the 6th-fret note. Move the 4th finger up to the 3rd string to play notes 6 and 8.

Track 63, 0:26

Minor arpeggio sequences using pattern #4

In the following figure, check out the ascending and descending sequences in 9th-position A minor.

This arpeggio pattern contains an out-of-position note on the 1st string. But to create a legato effect with alternate fingering, the stretch moves to places other than where the out-of-position note is.

For example, to play the 12 notes in the ascending sequence and sustain as long as possible between each note, write (lightly and with a pencil) these fingerings in the music: 4-3-**4**-2-(3)-(2)-1-(4)-(2)-**3**-**4**-(1). Plain numbers indicate the first time a finger is placed or played; bold numbers indicate a moved finger; and numbers in parentheses indicate that the finger is already being held down when the note is played.

In the descending version, as you may expect, the fingering is a little different: 4-1-2-**4**-(1)-(4)-3-(2)-(4)-(2)-**4**-(3). Note that the descending alternate-fingering scheme is a little more efficient; it has only two moved notes (indicated in bold) and six notes that are already in their held-down position when played (in parentheses). Compare that with the ascending version's three moved fingers and five held-down fingers.

Track 64, 0:00

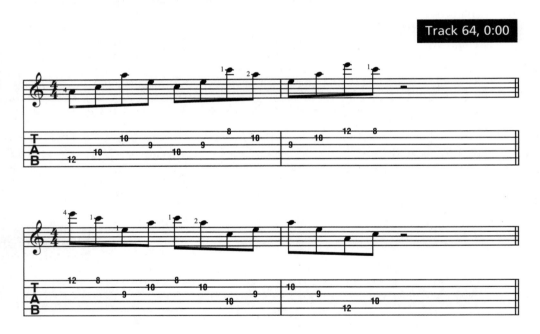

In the following figure are four-note ascending and descending sequences in 2nd-position D minor. To play the ascending version with a legato feel, try the following alternate fingering for the 12 notes: 4-1-2-4-2-3-1-3-2-1-4-2. What's interesting — and challenging — about this fingering is that each of your four fingers must move to play a new note in the sequence. So even though you're trying to hold down notes to increase sustain, you still have a lot of moving to do. To make things a little easier on yourself, use the 1st finger (instead of the 2nd) to play the last note. You'll have less of a stretch between the 4th and 2nd fingers — especially because this exercise is played in 1st position, where the frets are spaced widely apart.

Track 64, 0:20

Minor arpeggio sequences using pattern #5

Try the following pair of four-note ascending and descending sequences. They're in the key of E♭ minor in 1st position. The ascending version can be played pretty well with the fingering indicated. The only exception is the nasty 4th-fret jump between the 4th and 2nd strings.

If you want to eliminate this awkward string-hop — and create a legato effect in the process — consider using the following alternate fingering: Play the first four notes with the normal fingering. But on the fifth note, use the 3rd finger, not the 4th. Move your whole hand up to grab this note. (In other words, don't try to stretch for it from the 1st finger.) Use the 4th and 2nd fingers for the notes on the 2nd and 3rd strings, and use the 1st finger on the 1st string. The rest of the exercise plays out effortlessly.

Track 65, 0:00

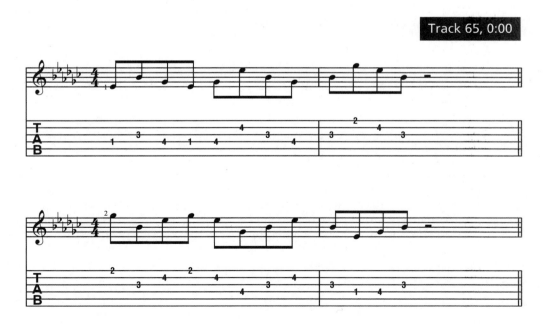

After you're comfortable with the previous set of sequences, move on to the following set, which is in 6th-position G♯ minor. Hold on to your hats, dear readers! These sequences are unique in that they can't be made more legato through alternate-fingering approaches. Yes, we want you to use the fingering as written! That's just the luck of how the sequence lays out sometimes. So play as is, and work for speed, fluidity, and quick memorization.

Track 65, 0:20

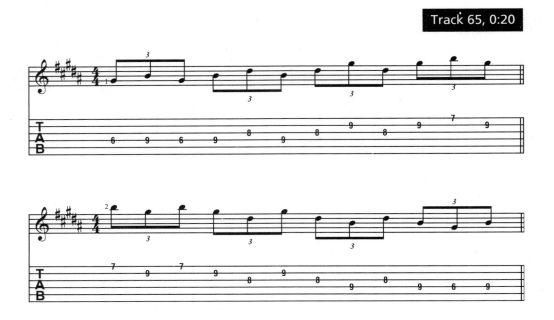

Tackling a Few Pieces Composed of Minor Arpeggio Sequences

The pieces we provide in the following sections feature minor arpeggio sequences drawn from classical composers Wolfgang Amadeus Mozart and Robert Schumann. Both pieces are fairly easy to play, and when you realize that many of the patterns can also be played out of a chord form, they're even easier. Try them both ways — using the fingering as required by the arpeggio patterns you practiced in Chapter 9 and with held-down chords and/or mini-barres.

"Mozart's Motif"

We conclude our three-part series on Mozart (for those of you keeping track of the pieces from Chapter 9) with a piece drawn from his Piano Sonata No. 1 in C Major. What's interesting here is that this excerpt uses sequences in two ways. You see the smaller, descending two-note sequences that progress upward by chord tones to the octave, and you also see the longer one-bar sequences (ten notes total) that occur between the measures. Mozart was really good with structure this way, so you can find elegant examples like this all through his music. Or maybe he just wanted to appear in *Guitar Exercises For Dummies*. Note that bar 7 has a major arpeggio, which leads nicely into the final bar.

For this piece, you use minor arpeggio patterns #1 and #3, and even though #1 normally starts on the 6th string and #4 starts on the 5th, here they both play the exact same string sequence (4-5-3-4-2-3-1-2-3-4). Also, you get to use major arpeggio patterns #2 and #4 from Chapter 8. So the piece is a good memory test of your arpeggio patterns, both major and minor. Make sure you can play those major arpeggios as confidently as you can your freshly mastered minor arpeggios.

Pieces composed of arpeggios are often played legato, and you're encouraged to try that here. Just don't let the notes ring through the rests that follow the sequences. Those last notes should be played short and crisp, according to the written rhythm.

Track 66

Schumann's "The Wild Horseman"

Robert Schumann was a brilliant but troubled composer from the Romantic era. His wife, Clara, was a famous pianist who performed many of her husband's works. Schumann felt that his small hands limited him as a pianist, so he devised a contraption to try to stretch out his hands. It ended up causing an injury that prevented him from performing, and many people speculate that out of bitterness he composed pieces that are fiendishly difficult to play.

But we're not that fiendish, so we chose one of his relatively easy pieces called "The Wild Horseman," and we adapted it for guitar. It derives its lilting, cheerful feel from the 6/8 meter. You can almost imagine a horse cantering to the beat. The first half of the piece is in A minor and uses minor arpeggio patterns #1 and #4. The second half has the same melody, but is transposed up to D minor. Rather than slide your hand up five frets, however, you stay in 5th position and use minor arpeggio patterns #3 and #1.

Even though the song is in a minor key, it isn't composed entirely of minor arpeggios. Some major arpeggios sneak in, too. Be sure to observe the score direction *D.C. (take 1st ending) al Fine,* which instructs you on performing the sections in the correct order.

You can practice this piece as much as you like, but please don't overdo it as Schumann did. We don't want you to hurt yourself while playing the guitar!

Track 67

Brightly, in 2

Chapter 11

Enhancing Your Playing with Seventh Chord Arpeggios

In This Chapter

▶ Playing dominant, minor, and major seventh chord arpeggios

▶ Performing pieces using seventh chord arpeggios

*Y*ou can approach the construction of a chord in many ways, but one of the simplest is to start with a scale and play every other note. For example, in the key of C, if you play C, E, and G — the 1, 3, and 5 in numerical terms — you produce a C major chord. Play C, E♭, and G (1, ♭3, 5), and you get a C minor chord. If you add the next note in the series, which is, numerically speaking, a 7 (in this case, B), you get a *seventh chord.* Seventh chords come in many different types, but they all have to have some form of 1, 3, 5, and 7.

Seventh chords sound richer and more complex than basic major and minor chords, and they're prevalent in many types of music, including jazz, pop, classical, rock, and blues. In this chapter, we focus on the three most common types of seventh chords: dominant seventh, minor seventh, and major seventh. Many more varieties of seventh chords exist, but they're more complex-sounding, so we stick with the ones that occur in many different types of music and crop up a lot.

In this chapter, we present each seventh chord arpeggio both in a neck diagram and in music and tab. You can use either one as a reference; sometimes it's just quicker to use one or the other. Because arpeggios are often related to chord forms, you may find it easier to look at the neck diagrams first.

After you memorize an arpeggio's fingering pattern, simply move it up or down the neck to a different starting note. Doing so produces other chord arpeggios. The sound of the chords stays the same, but as you switch positions, the key, or letter name, of the arpeggio changes. If you're not sure how the notes lay out on the fretboard, take a look at the guitar neck diagram on the Cheat Sheet that shows the letter names of all the frets on all six strings.

Practicing Dominant Seventh Chord Arpeggios

You can derive a dominant seventh chord in different ways, but here's how you should do it for now: Start with a major scale and play 1, 3, 5, ♭7. For example, in the key of C, if you play C, E, G, and B♭, you produce a C dominant seventh chord, or C7, for short.

As you work through the arpeggio exercises, play each one from low to high, slowly, loudly, and deliberately at first. After you've practiced an exercise a few times, play it faster and lighter. No matter how you're playing, however, be sure to maintain your starting tempo and dynamic level (loudness) throughout the arpeggio.

Dominant seventh chord arpeggio pattern #1

The following figure shows an A dominant seventh chord arpeggio in 5th position in both a neck diagram and in music and tab format. The *out-of-position notes* (or notes outside the four-fret span of the position) for this pattern occur at the two extremes of the fretboard — on the 6th and 1st strings. As a warm-up, jump from playing 1-4-1-4 on the 6th string to 1-4-1-4 on the 1st string, and back again. Note that your fingers naturally curl up at the 1st string and extend out at the 6th, so this is a good flexing exercise as well as a stretching one for your fingers.

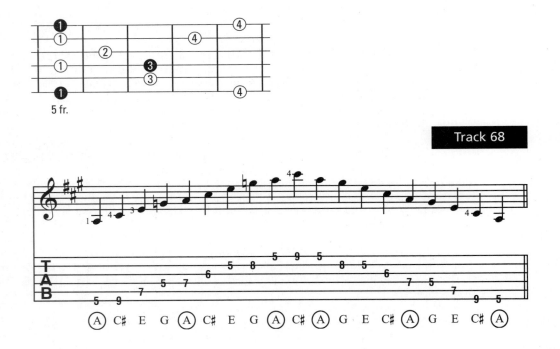

Track 68

This next figure shows an exercise in rhythm. It's in the key of B in 7th position. Try accenting the first and fifth notes of each measure, as they fall on the strong beats in 4/4 (beats 1 and 3).

Dominant seventh chord arpeggio pattern #2

The following figure shows the neck diagram and corresponding music and tab for dominant seventh chord arpeggio pattern #2 in the key of C. The first three notes of the pattern are all on different strings, requiring a bit of right-hand practice if you're playing with a pick. Consider switching to fingerstyle for this exercise, which allows you to focus on the left hand without having to worry about mastering a tricky right-hand alternate-picking pattern that may slow you down. To make sure you can play the hard parts of this pattern as well as the not-so-hard parts, try practicing just the first three notes eight times in a row before playing through the entire pattern.

To make this pattern a bit easier, you can flatten your 1st finger to play the consecutive notes on the 3rd and 2nd strings, which both occur at the same fret (the 5th). Think of this flattened 1st finger as a *mini-barre* (a partial barre that covers just two or three strings). This technique is especially helpful if you want to create a more *legato* (smooth and connected) sound between the notes.

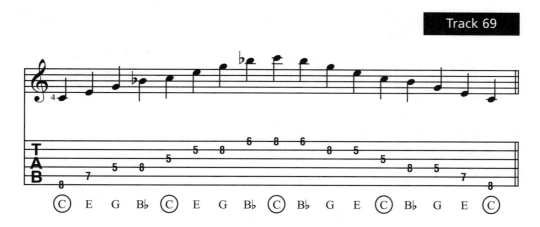

When you're ready, try the exercise in the following figure. It's in the key of A in 2nd position. Playing dominant seventh chord arpeggios in triplets is a great way to fill out the chords in a swing of shuffle blues, so work on really digging into the notes here with feeling.

Dominant seventh chord arpeggio pattern #3

The patterns in the previous few sections have a range of at least two octaves. Dominant seventh chord arpeggio patterns #3, #4, and #5, on the other hand, span a bit less than two octaves. With fewer notes available in a position, you might consider these for shorter passages — those where you don't need to play an entire neck width's worth of notes to fill the space. Refer to the following figure to see the neck diagram and the corresponding music and tab of dominant seventh chord arpeggio pattern #3, which is in the key of D here.

Two alternate fingering opportunities exist here: The first is to play the 4th string note with the 2nd finger, not the 3rd as is indicated. The second opportunity is to play the 2nd string note with the 4th finger (not the 3rd). This way you don't have to use the same finger two times in a row (where the finger has to "hop" across the string, which is a little awkward). Practice both alternate-fingering substitutions as well as the written fingering to ensure that you can make an informed choice as to which of the four combinations you prefer. Eight times through with each of the four combinations (32 times total) ought to do it!

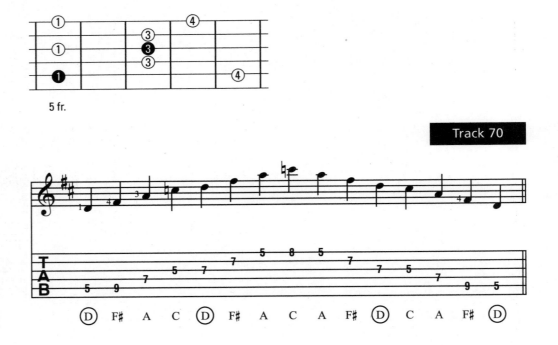

Play the exercise in the following figure, which is in the key of E in 7th position. For ease of playing and to avoid the awkwardness that string-hopping creates, try using both of these alternate-fingering substitutions for this one: the 2nd finger on the 4th string, and the 4th finger on the 2nd string.

Dominant seventh chord arpeggio pattern #4

To see the neck diagram and corresponding music and tab for dominant seventh chord arpeggio pattern #4 in 5th position in the key of F, check out the following figure. Notice that with this pattern, as in dominant seventh chord pattern #2, you have to play the first three notes on different strings. This makes the first half of the pattern a little trickier than the second — especially if you're alternate picking, where changing strings after every note requires more practice. So practice the first four notes of this pattern in isolation a few times before running through the entire pattern.

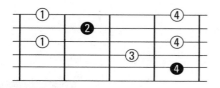

5 fr.

Track 71

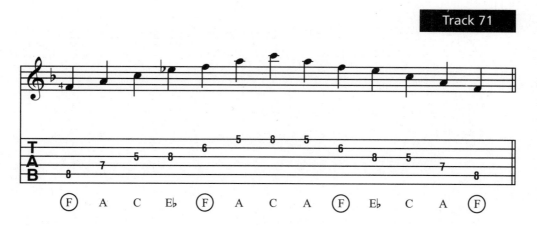

(F)   A   C   E♭   (F)   A   C   A   (F)   E♭   C   A   (F)

When you're ready for some practice, try the following exercise in rhythm, which is in the key of D in 2nd position. Just for fun, try playing this exercise by holding down all your fingers except the 4th, including a 1st-finger barre across the top three strings. When you do this, only the 4th finger needs to move in order to play all the notes in the arpeggio. You not only get to isolate the 4th finger from the other three fixed fingers, but you also get to hear how the pattern sounds with a very legato treatment.

Dominant seventh chord arpeggio pattern #5

Refer to the following figure to see the neck diagram and corresponding music and tab for dominant seventh chord arpeggio pattern #5 in 5th position in the key of G. This pattern poses some unusual uses for the 2nd, 3rd, and 4th fingers, and many players would play this using four alternate fingers (described in the following exercise). But for now, practice this pattern as written to get a feel for the way fingers 2, 3, and 4 would be used in a classic sense.

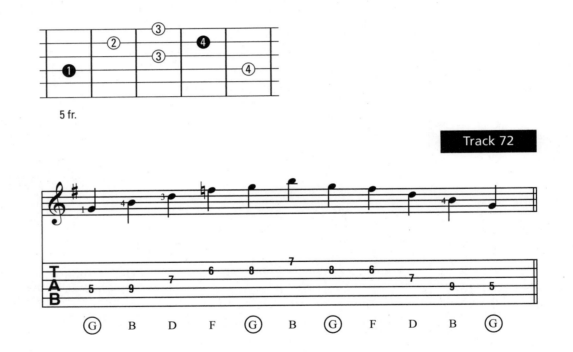

Track 72

As practice, try the exercise in the following figure. It shows dominant arpeggio pattern #5 in the key of A in 7th position. Play the first two notes with the fingerings as written (1 and 4). But then use the following fingerings, which are all deviations from the original: 2nd finger on the 3rd string, 1st finger on the 2nd string followed by the 3rd finger on the 2nd string, and 2nd finger on the 1st string. If you find it more comfortable, feel free to play pattern #5 this way. It's as if the starting finger 1, not the stretched-up 4th finger, is out of position. If you started with the 4th finger, all the other alternate fingerings would be the correct ones! That's one of the great things about guitar: There's no one way to play something, and what's right for you may be something entirely different from the "correct" way.

Putting Your Fingers to Work with Minor Seventh Chord Arpeggios

Minor seventh chords can be derived in different ways, but one way is to start with a major scale and play 1, ♭3, 5, ♭7. So in the key of C, a Cm7 (C minor seven) chord is spelled C, E♭, G, B♭.

When you're ready to practice the arpeggios in this section, be sure to play each from low to high slowly, loudly, and deliberately at first. Then play it faster and lighter. Just be sure to maintain your starting tempo and dynamic level throughout the arpeggio.

Minor seventh chord arpeggio pattern #1

The following figure shows an A minor seventh chord arpeggio in 5th position in both a neck diagram and in music and tab. There's just one spot where you may consider a mini-barre substitution for a same-finger hop across two strings: between the 3rd and 2nd strings. Try playing these consecutive 1st-finger-fretted strings as a mini-barre, both ascending and descending.

Before moving on, practice both methods — the 1st-finger hop and the mini-barre — an equal number of times to see which feels more comfortable.

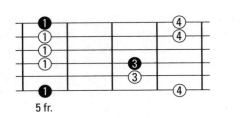

5 fr.

Track 73

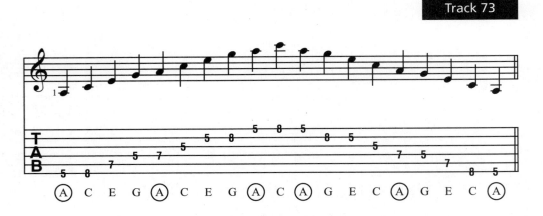

Ⓐ C E G Ⓐ C E G Ⓐ C Ⓐ G E C Ⓐ G E C Ⓐ

Here's an exercise in rhythm for you to practice. It's in the key of G minor in 3rd position. A great trick for playing legato passages in minor seventh chord arpeggio pattern #1 is to barre all six strings with the 1st finger and keep it anchored. Then selectively add the 4th and 3rd fingers (you don't use the 2nd finger at all in this pattern) where appropriate. This requires a little more flexibility in your hand than if you play all the 1st-finger notes with the fingertip, but the results are definitely worth it; it's a very economical way to play an arpeggio.

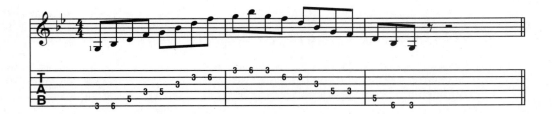

Minor seventh chord arpeggio pattern #2

Because minor seventh chord arpeggio pattern #2 relies heavily on the 4th finger (which is weaker than the others), it isn't quite as easy to play as minor seventh chord arpeggio pattern #1. But as an option, you can flatten your 4th finger to play the consecutive notes on the 3rd and 2nd strings, which occur at the same fret (the 8th in this example). This is especially helpful if you want to create a more legato sound between the notes.

The following figure shows the neck diagram and corresponding music and tab for minor seventh chord arpeggio pattern #2 in the key of C minor. Practice this pattern using both the written fingering and the suggested mini-barre fingering that we mention in the previous paragraph. See if you can make them indistinguishable from each other. Then try to fool another guitar player in a blind test!

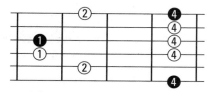

5 fr.

Track 74

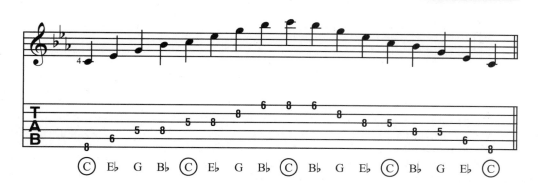

When you're ready for some practice, give the exercise in the following figure a try. It's in the key of B minor in 7th position. As with all triplets, accent the first note in each group to help emphasize the three-note groupings. However, remember that because seventh chords have four notes in them, various chord tones rotate (and thus receive the accent) as you play through the sequence. Consider this rotation a good thing, because it means that none of the notes will feel neglected! As you play the following exercise, you accent, in order, B (6th string), A (4th string), F♯ (2nd string), A (1st string), B (3rd string), and D (5th string) — all different pitches, each on a different string. How cool is that?

Minor seventh chord arpeggio pattern #3

The minor seventh chord arpeggio patterns in the previous two sections have a range of at least two octaves. However, minor seventh chord arpeggio patterns #3, #4, and #5 span a bit less than two octaves. So you have fewer notes with which to illustrate a minor seventh idea using pattern #3. But don't worry. You can fill the space by repeating notes (by double striking them), switching directions more often, or repeating groups of notes.

To see the neck diagram and corresponding music and tab for minor seventh chord arpeggio pattern #3 in 5th position in the key of D minor, check out the following figure. This is a well behaved pattern, at least in fingering terms, because it not only contains no out-of-position notes (which means no stretching!), but you also don't need to employ any alternate fingerings. It just lies perfectly under your fingers. Practice this pattern with both a legato and staccato feel (alternating between the two) about eight times each to make sure you can produce both effects using identical fingering.

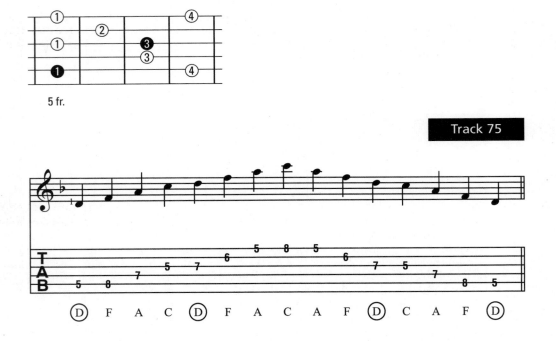

Here's an exercise you can try that's in the key of F♯ minor in 9th position. Even though you don't have to turn your 1st finger into a barre to play this exercise, try it anyway, and see how you can create a sustained, harp-like sound by letting the strings ring as long as possible. Holding your 1st finger in a fixed position while moving the 2nd, 3rd, and 4th fingers to fret the various notes in the pattern helps develop finger independence, too.

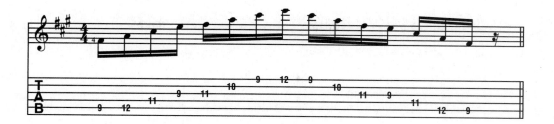

Minor seventh chord arpeggio pattern #4

The following figure shows the neck diagram and corresponding music and tab for minor seventh chord arpeggio pattern #4 in the key of F minor. It includes an out-of-position note on the 1st string. Because this note occurs one fret below (lower on the neck) where the finger naturally falls, you must stretch down (toward the nut) with your 1st finger to reach it.

 The downward stretch is less common in out-of-position playing than the upward stretch, so try isolating just the stretch by playing the top three notes of the pattern starting from the 2nd string. Practice this three-note segment up and down eight times before playing through the entire pattern.

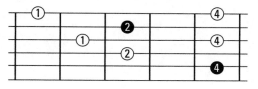

4 fr.

Track 76

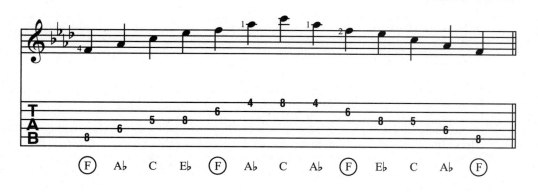

For practice, we provide the following exercise, which is in the key of E minor in 4th position. For a good stretching workout between your 2nd and 1st fingers, leave your 2nd finger on the 2nd string (and let the string ring out) as you play the 1st string notes. This technique really tugs apart those 1st and 2nd fingers and is good for getting limber in a hurry!

Minor seventh chord arpeggio pattern #5

The following figure shows the neck diagram and corresponding music and tab for minor seventh chord arpeggio pattern #5 in the key of G minor. This pattern emphasizes the 2nd, 3rd, and 4th fingers, which are traditionally a weaker set than the 1st, 2nd, and 3rd fingers. So it's a great pattern to get the "B Team" up to snuff. Practice pattern #5 after you've been playing a lot of barre chords (which give the 1st finger a workout), and isolate the move between the 4th and 2nd fingers on the top two strings if this motion feels less familiar or comfortable than other combinations of fingers.

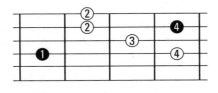

5 fr.

Track 77

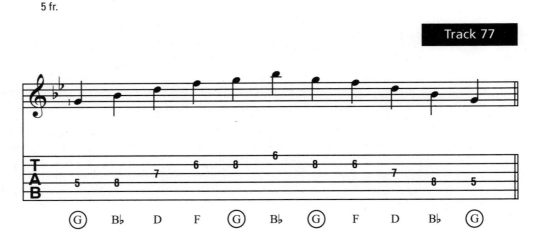

When you're ready for some practice, check out the following exercise, which is in the key of B♭ minor in 8th position. Notice that an eighth rest ends the measure. This rest may leave you with the feeling that the exercise ended a bit short or even sounds truncated. But if you fill in that eighth rest with a played note, you can create a repeatable loop that allows you to easily practice the pattern over and over. For that missing note, simply re-play the note before the last one — the 11th fret on the 4th string. As you loop the pattern, apply your accents to the first note of each triplet grouping.

Running Through the Major Seventh Chord Arpeggios

As with the dominant and minor seventh chords, you can derive a major seventh chord in many different ways. One way is to start with a major scale and play 1, 3, 5, 7. So in the key of C, a Cmaj7 (C major seven) chord is spelled C, E, G, B.

Play each arpeggio in this section from low to high slowly, loudly, and deliberately at first. After practicing a few rounds, play each one faster and lighter. No matter what, be sure to maintain your starting tempo and dynamic level throughout the arpeggio.

Major seventh chord arpeggio pattern #1

The following figure shows an A major seventh chord arpeggio in 5th position in both a neck diagram and in music and tab. Major seventh chord arpeggio pattern #1 includes three out-of-position notes — on the 6th, 2nd, and 1st strings. You have to stretch up (toward the bridge) with your 4th finger to reach these notes, because they occur one fret above (higher on the neck) where the finger naturally falls.

Mastering major seventh chord arpeggios is important because they outline the notes of the tonic seventh chord of a major key. No matter what seventh chords you encounter in a song that provide arpeggio opportunities, the tonic major seventh chord will almost certainly be one of them. (The one exception to the tonic seventh chord being a major seventh chord is in blues, which normally employs all dominant seventh chords.) So practice this pattern at least eight times through, or until you feel as comfortable with it as any other arpeggio in your repertoire.

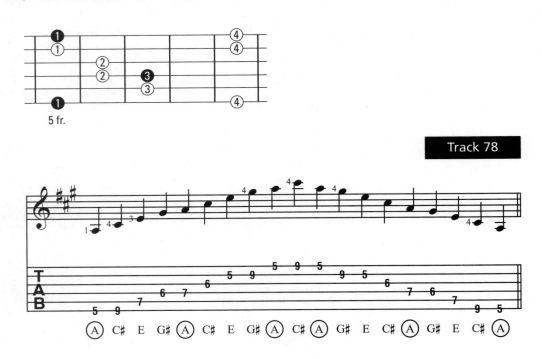

Track 78

The following is an exercise in rhythm in 8th-position C major.

In a major seventh chord arpeggio, the seventh is a half step away from the root, and so it's powerfully drawn back to the root. Here's a good habit to get into: Whenever you play major seventh arpeggios, always end on the root, not on the seventh.

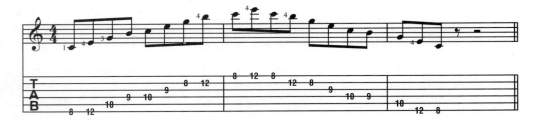

Major seventh chord arpeggio pattern #2

Refer to the following figure to see the neck diagram and corresponding music and tab for major seventh chord arpeggio pattern #2 in the key of C. The middle part of this pattern can be tricky, so create a mini exercise-within-an-exercise by playing just the notes on the 4th, 3rd, and 2nd strings ascending in a five-note loop that goes, by fingers, 1-4-1-1-4. Then go back down again. Practice this loop in isolation at least four times before running the entire pattern up and down.

You can flatten your 1st finger to play the consecutive notes on the 3rd and 2nd strings, which both occur at the same fret (the 5th in this example). Use this technique when you want to create a more legato sound between the notes.

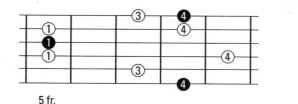

5 fr.

Track 79

Take a look at the following figure for some practice. This exercise is in the key of D in 7th position. You may notice that this pattern doesn't use the 2nd finger at all, so try watching that finger throughout the pattern to make sure it stays relaxed and hovering above the 8th fret — even during those stretches when the 4th finger reaches the 11th-fret note on the 4th string.

Major seventh chord arpeggio pattern #3

The patterns in the previous few sections have a range of at least two octaves. Major seventh chord arpeggio patterns #3, #4, and #5, on the other hand, span a bit less than two octaves. With a short pattern like #3, you may find yourself having to repeat notes to fill out an idea for a given arpeggio. Repeating notes is okay, but it means you have to think more creatively than when simply running a long pattern.

In the following figure are the neck diagram and the corresponding music and tab for major seventh chord arpeggio pattern #3 in the key of D.

This pattern can be a tricky one to master because it has two out-of-position stretches *and* a mini-barre option between the 3rd and 2nd strings. But because the pattern is relatively short, you don't need to isolate the passages. Instead you just have to run the pattern in its entirety until you can effectively execute the challenging aspects as smoothly as the straightforward ones. It may mean that you have to practice this pattern more times than another easier pattern — say, 12 or 16 times. But arpeggio patterns are like children: You love and treat them equally even though some are more "difficult" than others.

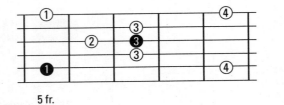

Track 80

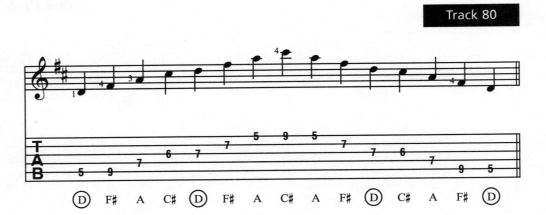

Try your hand at the exercise in the following figure, which is in the key of B. This pattern is placed in 2nd position — the second lowest possible on the neck — and it includes two stretches on widely separated strings. So, as you can imagine, it's an ideal stretching exercise. The great thing about this exercise is that you aren't just stretching your fingers and the span of your hand — you're also producing a major seventh chord arpeggio and, if you so choose, using a mini-barre substitution. File this one under the efficient finger exercises category!

Major seventh chord arpeggio pattern #4

The following figure shows the neck diagram and corresponding music and tab for major seventh chord arpeggio pattern #4 in the key of F. This pattern invites only one alternate approach — a mini-barre with your 1st finger between the 3rd and 2nd strings. You may not need to practice this mini-barre as much as the ones that occur in other patterns, but make sure you can play the entire pattern at least four times through perfectly, and try alternating between a legato and staccato feel for good measure.

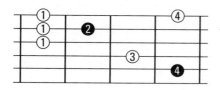

5 fr.

Track 81

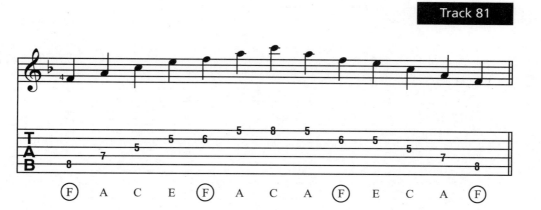

Try your hand at the following exercise, which is in the key of G. In 7th position, where this exercise is placed, everything becomes easier, including mini-barre substitutions. So try playing this exercise at a brisk clip.

What you may discover is that while the left hand poses no problems, playing four notes in a row each on a different string can be a challenge for the right hand — especially at fast tempos. We have two solutions for you. The first is to simply slow down and work up speed gradually. And the second is this: If you started out playing with a pick, go to fingerstyle, which makes consecutive-string playing a little easier than alternate picking.

Major seventh chord arpeggio pattern #5

The following figure shows the neck diagram and corresponding music and tab for major seventh chord arpeggio pattern #5 in the key of G. In addition to an out-of-position note, you have the opportunity to employ several alternate fingering solutions. Here's one to try: Instead of using the 3rd finger (either with the tip or as a mini-barre) on the 3rd, 2nd, and 1st strings, bring up your 1st finger and plant it across the first three strings at the 7th fret immediately after you leave the first note of the exercise. Keep it there until the very last moment when you have to move it back to the starting note on the 4th string, 5th fret. Practice the move of shifting your 1st finger up two frets and then back down again until the pattern is as comfortable — or more so! — than the original fingering.

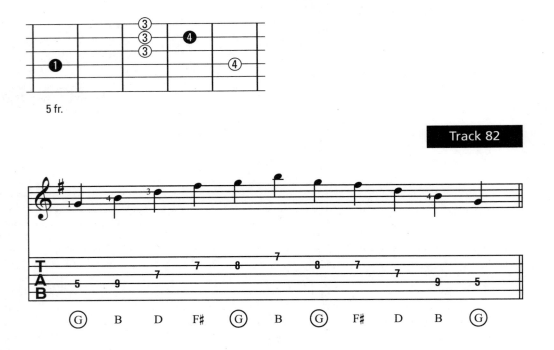

5 fr.

Track 82

Now check out this exercise, which is in the key of F♯ in 4th position. This exercise is only one fret lower than the previous pattern, where you practiced the original and alternate fingerings. So what changes? We bet that you practiced the previous pattern in divisions where the notes came two or four to the beat. Here, however, you have to think of grouping the notes in threes, because this exercise is in triplets. Because this pattern is so short, you may not even really get the triplet feel by playing this only one time through. So, we suggest that you employ the trick applied in minor seventh chord arpeggio pattern #5, where you replace the final rest with the next-to-last note of the exercise (in this case, the 4th string, 8th fret). Loop the exercise several times to hear the triplet feel establishing itself. Notice that the accent falls on a different chord tone and string every time. That's the beat rotation effect that occurs when you group a four-note chord pattern over a rhythmic grouping of three. Remember to apply those accents on the first note of each group of three.

Applying Seventh Chord Arpeggios to Some Famous Pieces

When you leave the realm of simple major and minor chords and delve into music that uses seventh chords, a new world of harmonic colors opens up. So in this section, we elevate your practice a notch by including some actual pieces that use seventh chord arpeggios. We include two pieces that use seventh chords to provide rich-sounding harmonies. One is from the Romantic era and the other is from the pre-Modern era. Many different types of music rely heavily on seventh chords, including jazz, rock, blues, and world music.

Schubert's "Ave Maria"

There are two famous versions of "Ave Maria" — one by Bach and Gounod and one by Schubert. We've chosen the latter to show how a dominant seventh chord arpeggio goes well with major and minor arpeggios. (Don't worry; we give Bach's "Ave Maria" equal time in Chapter 12.) Schubert's piece is made up of mostly major and minor chords, but when the dominant seventh chord arpeggios come in, they almost announce themselves. They hint that the music is going to change, or at least provide something unexpected and interesting.

In the music for Schubert's "Ave Maria" (shown in the following figure), we indicate the different arpeggio patterns used — eight different ones in all, including dominant seventh patterns #1, #2, #4, and #5. Almost all the major and minor arpeggios can be played out of chord forms. If you recognize which forms those are (your hand will naturally create them if you simply hold down your 1st finger as a barre), you're welcome to employ them. Holding down a chord form, or even part of one, helps sustain the notes, which is a desired effect in this piece.

We supply the correct fingering according to the patterns presented in this chapter, but you can often find alternate ways to play the arpeggios. For example, in bar 7, try fingering the first four notes with the 3rd, 4th, 1st, and 4th fingers, respectively. You just have to move the 4th finger from the 4th string to the 2nd in time to play that fourth note. In bars 8 and 9, you can play both measures comfortably by barring first the 4th fret and then the 5th with your 1st finger. See how many more barring or efficient fingering moves you can find.

Track 83

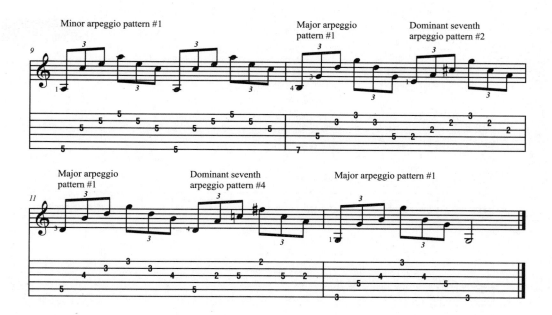

Fauré's "Pavane"

Gabriel Fauré was a French composer who wrote beautiful pieces using a rich palette of harmonic material, much of it based on seventh chords. In "Pavane," which is quite a haunting piece, he uses major seventh, minor seventh, and dominant seventh chords with great frequency. (A *pavane*, by the way, is a slow and stately processional dance.)

In the music to Fauré's "Pavane," shown in the following figure, we label the different arpeggio patterns used. There are 14 in all, including various forms of the three types of seventh chords — dominant seventh, minor seventh, and major seventh.

In this piece, as in Schubert's "Ave Maria" from the previous section, you can find many opportunities to play legato by employing barres with your 1st and 3rd fingers. You can also play by holding down your fretting fingers for as long as you can — or at least until the held finger must move to fret another string. For example, you can play all the arpeggios in bars 2 through 5 using held-down chords.

The reason you use chords is that they make arpeggios sound more legato, and they require little or no left-hand movement. You form a chord just before the first note in each half of the measure and hold it there for two beats. Then you simply play the notes of the arpeggio with your right hand while keeping your left hand stationary, allowing the strings to ring.

Not all of the arpeggios can be played using barres and held fingers. Some you must play by fingering each note in a separate motion (the way the arpeggios are presented in this chapter). So you must master both skills — employing barres and held-down fingers, and fingering each note separately — to play the arpeggios in this song to their best effect.

Track 84

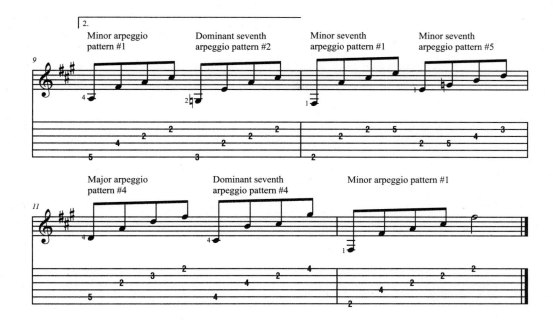

Chapter 12

Trying Your Hand at Seventh Chord Arpeggio Sequences

*I*n this chapter, you play arpeggio sequences composed of the notes of the three different seventh chords we discuss in Chapter 11 — the dominant seventh chord, the minor seventh chord, and the major seventh chord.

With seventh chord arpeggio sequences, you face many of the same challenges served up by straight seventh chord arpeggios, including playing the same fret on consecutive strings and stretching for *out-of-position notes* (notes that don't fall within the four-fret span defined by the position and that require stretches by the 1st or 4th finger to play). You're welcome to try alternate fingerings for the tricky situations, but be sure you can get back on track with the normal fingering if you (or a teacher) decide on an alternate fingering for a certain passage. We provide additional fingerings throughout this chapter whenever a sequence takes you out of position so that you can get back into position.

Just as in your arpeggio work, you should move all the sequences presented in this chapter up and down the neck to produce other chord arpeggio sequences. Check the Cheat Sheet to find the correct starting note for any given arpeggio.

Taking On Dominant Seventh Chord Arpeggio Sequences

In this section, we help you become familiar with dominant seventh chord arpeggio sequences. These sequences are helpful because having experience with a variety of sequences better prepares you for actual passages that occur in "real music" (you know, composed pieces, rather than just exercises). Make sure that arpeggio sequences are as much a part of your practice routine as scales, scale sequences, and arpeggios. Guitar players play chords as much as single notes, and arpeggio sequences bridge the two worlds of chords and melodies.

Dominant seventh chord arpeggio sequence using pattern #1

The following figure shows four-note ascending and descending sequences in the key of G in 3rd position. As an alternate fingering option, try holding down your 1st finger as a barre, and then pre-set and hold your 3rd and 2nd fingers on the 5th and 3rd strings as well. This way you can play the whole sequence moving just your 4th finger while keeping the rest of your fingers stationary.

The stretch of the 4th finger requires a little more flexibility this way than if you play the exercise as all single notes. So you take extra care in warming up (see Chapter 2) if you're coming to this sequence "cold."

Track 85, 0:00

Dominant seventh chord arpeggio sequence using pattern #2

The following figure shows three-note ascending and descending sequences in the key of E in 9th position. Because the sequences are organized in three-note groupings and the rhythms are a steady flow of triplets, the pattern coincides evenly with the rhythms. So you can play the ascending and descending versions back to back if you start the descending version on beat 4 of the last bar of the ascending version.

For a good fingering option, form a *mini-barre* (a partial barre that covers just two or three strings) with your 1st finger and place it on the 3rd and 2nd strings. Play those higher-string notes *legato* (smooth and connected) while keeping the notes on the lowest three strings shorter and more detached sounding.

Track 85, 0:23

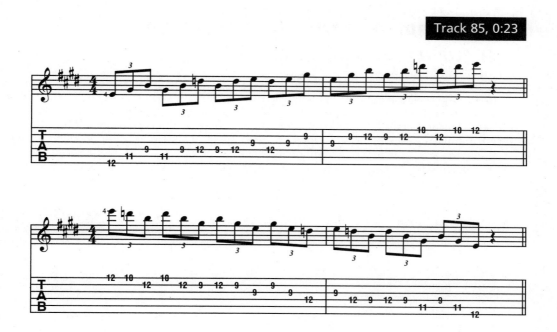

Dominant seventh chord arpeggio sequence using pattern #3

Take a look at the following figure, which shows four-note ascending and descending sequences in the key of C in 3rd position. These sequences involve many same-fret string jumps, which are usually played either with a quick "hop" of the same finger to the next string or with a mini-barre. But in this case, you can play all the same-fret notes by using other fingers. Play note 12 (4th string, 5th fret) using the 2nd finger (not the 3rd) and play note 15 (2nd string, 5th fret) using the 4th finger. This substitution scheme works for both the ascending and descending versions, and it's actually a lot of fun to play!

Track 85, 0:51

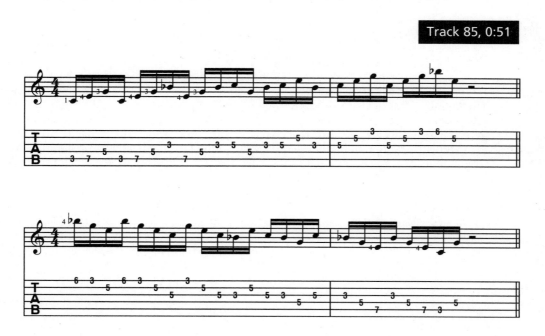

Dominant seventh chord arpeggio sequence using pattern #4

When you're ready for some more practice, check out the following figure. It shows four-note ascending and descending sequences in the key of F♯ in 6th position. You have to play some wide skips in this pattern, and the string skipping doesn't make it any easier. But the good news is that you don't have to consider any alternate fingering options. This pattern plays best with only one fingering — the one indicated. Try playing this one *staccato* — where all the notes are short, crisp, and detached from one another — and then lift the previous finger up (causing it to deaden the string) as you press down the new one. Think of this one as your "whack-a-mole" sequence.

Track 85, 1:19

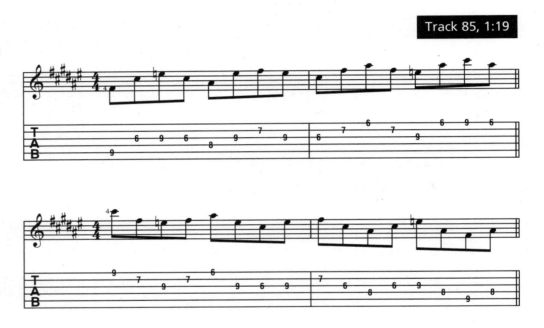

Dominant seventh chord arpeggio sequence using pattern #5

The following figure shows three-note ascending and descending sequences in the key of F in 3rd position. This pattern is an unusual one because you can use an alternate fingering scheme that replaces the provided fingering on three of the four strings. Try playing this exercise with the 2nd, 1st, and 3rd fingers substituted for the 3rd, 2nd, and 4th fingers on the top three strings. Retain the original fingering only for the 4th string. Most people find this easier than the given fingering. Practice the exercise both ways at least eight times (or until both are comfortable) to see which way you prefer.

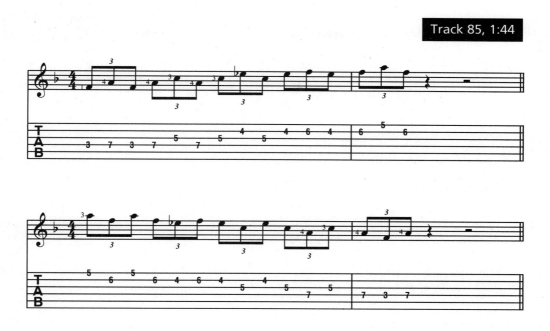

Adding Minor Seventh Chord Arpeggio Sequences to Your Collection

If you're ready to practice minor seventh chord arpeggio sequences, this is the section for you. After practicing these, your fingers will know what to do whenever you run into a minor seventh chord that requires single-note playing. And there are a lot of those in music!

In some types of music, particularly jazz, minor seventh chord arpeggio sequences occur with more frequency than many other types of seventh chord arpeggio sequences. So playing minor seventh chords better prepares you for playing jazz, or music that involves jazz-type stylings (such as pop songs by Norah Jones and John Mayer, who like to employ jazz chords). Play the minor seventh chord arpeggio sequences in the following sections along with minor seventh chord arpeggios (in Chapter 11) to make sure you get a thorough workout with minor seventh material.

Minor seventh chord arpeggio sequence using pattern #1

Refer to the following figure for practice. It shows four-note ascending and descending sequences in the key of B minor in 7th position. Start out the ascending version playing the notes with your fingertips (substituting the 4th finger for the 3rd on the tenth note, if you like), and then flatten out your 1st finger to play the remainder of the exercise with a 1st-finger mini-barre. You can use the 4th finger as a mini-barre for notes 13 and 14 in bar 2, creating a double mini-barre between your 1st and 4th finger. Don't worry, this is all perfectly legal!

Track 86, 0:00

Minor seventh chord arpeggio sequence using pattern #2

Take a look at the following figure, which shows four-note ascending and descending sequences in the key of A minor in 2nd position. An interesting alternate-fingering situation presents itself in bar 2 of the ascending version. Instead of playing a mini-barre for notes 5, 6, and 7 (all played at the 5th fret), play these notes with the 2nd, 3rd, and 4th fingers; play the 1st string with your 1st finger.

This pattern shows that you don't have to resort to a mini-barre every time you see the same fret across multiple strings. If the frets are large enough, as they are when they're this far down the neck (2nd position), you can play them easily with individual fingers.

Track 86, 0:31

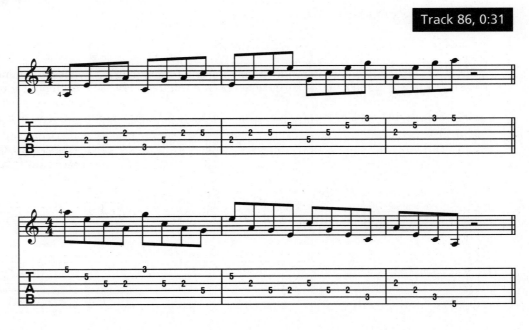

Minor seventh chord arpeggio sequence using pattern #3

When you're ready to try this pattern, check out the following figure, which consists of ascending and descending sequences in C minor in 3rd position. Because these sequences are so short (only nine notes long), try playing them back to back, with no break (or rest) in between. To do this, play the first note of the descending version at bar 1, beat 4, of the ascending version, where the quarter rest is now.

You'll have to *double-strike* (that is, play twice in a row) the top note, but that's okay. Play the second of these double strikes with more force than the first. Doing so creates an accent that helps delineate the second note from the first and emphasize the strong part of the beat.

Track 86, 1:00

Minor seventh chord arpeggio sequence using pattern #4

The following figure shows four-note ascending and descending sequences in G minor in 7th position. These sequences work well when played legato, so try to let each note sound as long as possible before you have to move a finger to play a new note. Because the pattern is fairly high up the neck, even the out-of-position stretch is fairly comfortable to hold.

Track 86, 1:18

Minor seventh chord arpeggio sequence using pattern #5

The following figure shows ascending and descending sequences in the key of E minor in 2nd position. This pattern is a short and easily managed one, and the left-hand fingers can pretty much take care of themselves on this one. However, you have one opportunity to try a novel approach on the last two notes of the ascending version. Play note 7 on the 2nd string normally (with the 2nd-finger fingertip). Then let your 2nd finger form a mini-barre across the top two strings to grab the last note (on the 1st string).

 This technique is different from applying a mini-barre, which goes down once (for the first note) and stays still while the 2nd, barred note is played. Here, you're flattening the finger quickly, in time with the music, just as the last note is played. It's a lot of fun to do, and you can get consistent, clean results once you master it.

Track 86, 1:43

Practicing Major Seventh Chord Arpeggio Sequences

This section is your gateway to becoming great at major seventh chord arpeggio sequences. Why would you want to master these? Because they're the ones you want first on the scene when the music to a major seventh chord goes missing! Seriously, though, you can play major seventh chord arpeggios in any accompaniment situation where single notes are needed (such as in jazz tunes and sophisticated pop songs) and all you have is a major seventh chord symbol to go by. A major seventh chord sounds even more "jazzy" than a minor seventh chord.

Play the patterns and exercises in the following sections along with your major scales and major scale sequences, and work to get the arpeggios and the arpeggio sequences as smooth sounding as your scales and scale sequences.

Major seventh chord arpeggio sequence using pattern #1

When you're ready to practice pattern #1, refer to the following figure, which shows three-note ascending and descending sequences in the key of B in 7th position. Are you practicing your descending exercises as often as your ascending ones? Remember that these figures are meant to be played in *pairs*. So always follow — immediately — the ascending version with the descending one to stay musically balanced. This is true of scale sequences, too.

Track 87, 0:00

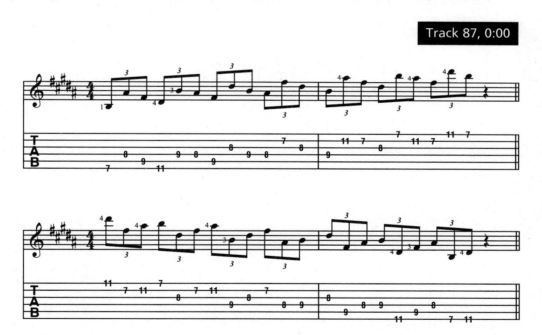

Major seventh chord arpeggio sequence using pattern #2

The ascending and descending exercises in the following figure consist of a four-note sequence in 6th-position Db, which is an unusual guitar key. But because it's a movable pattern, you can play it with the same ease as major seventh chord arpeggio sequence #2 in C, which is only one fret away and has no sharps or flats! Be sure that you move your patterns around the neck and call out the starting notes (which are the tonic or root, depending on the type of pattern) as you begin playing them. When you're a guitar player it's easy to change movable patterns around, but you still have to know what key you're in or what arpeggio you're playing.

Track 87, 0:26

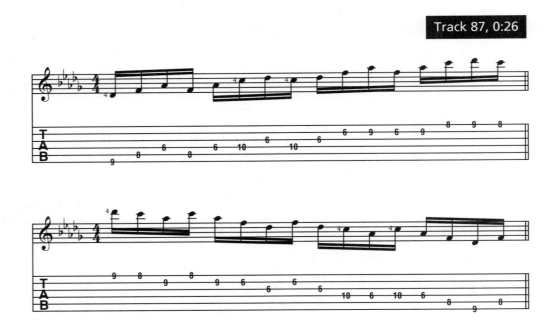

Major seventh chord arpeggio sequence using pattern #3

Check out the following figure, which shows a pair of ascending and descending exercises using a four-note sequence in the key of E in 7th position. The 4th, 3rd, and 2nd strings have you jumping around quite a bit as your fingers try to get out of the way of the coming notes.

 If you have trouble making this particular exercise sound smooth, try going back to the corresponding major seventh chord arpeggio in Chapter 11. Really drill those notes into your memory. It's easier to memorize the notes in an arpeggio than in an arpeggio sequence. And remember that you may have to go back to the basics every once in a while, especially when confronting more difficult exercises.

Track 87, 0:49

Major seventh chord arpeggio sequence using pattern #4

The following figure shows three-note ascending and descending sequences in what *would be* the very user-unfriendly key of G♭ (here placed in 6th position). However, you're using movable patterns, so six flats in the key signature is like water off a duck's back to you. As always, play the ascending version back to back with its descending counterpart. Playing the two exercises without a break in between helps you to better recognize the symmetry between the two versions, and it aids your memory in finding the correct notes on the fretboard — regardless of the direction you're going.

Track 87, 1:19

Major seventh chord arpeggio sequence using pattern #5

The following figure shows four-note ascending and descending exercises in the key of A in 7th position. These sequences are relatively short (three beats long), so try playing them as one continuous piece of music. To do this successfully, start the descending sequence at beat 4 of the ascending sequence — where the quarter rest is. You'll have to double-strike the high (1st string) note, but you can add an accent on the second strike to help emphasize the starting note of the descending sequence.

Here's one alternate fingering possibility for this pattern: Play the 3rd and 2nd strings with the 2nd and 3rd fingers, respectively. This allows you to produce a nice legato sound and keep your fingers fairly stationary on the neck. (Personally, we don't like to move unless we absolutely *have* to.) Keep in mind that fingering the exercises this way does create a little bit of a stretch between the 1st and 2nd fingers, but it isn't too bad here, because you're fairly high up on the neck.

Alternate fingerings may work well in one position but not others. It's based largely on the size of the frets, which get narrower — and the distance between them correspondingly smaller — the higher up the neck you go. Seventh position is considered a high position, because you're often playing notes up to and including the 11th fret.

Track 87, 1:41

Playing Pieces with Seventh Chord Arpeggio Sequences

When you encounter actual pieces of music, you discover that there isn't a whole lot of difference between the seventh chord arpeggios you find in Chapter 11 and the seventh chord arpeggio sequences you find here in this chapter. So we've made an effort to imbue the guitar accompaniment figures in the following two pieces with a real sense of "sequence-ness."

Liszt's "Liebestraum"

Franz Liszt was a Hungarian-born German Romantic composer who was also a virtuoso pianist — some say the greatest pianist of all time. He enjoyed fame during his lifetime, hung out with Chopin and Mendelssohn, and was father-in-law to the great opera composer Richard Wagner.

The piece we've chosen to provide you with a workout in seventh chord arpeggio sequences is one of Liszt's slower pieces, "Liebestraum." This piece, which means "dream of love," is shown in the following figure. Its slow-moving, static melody helps highlight the interesting flavorful chords Liszt places behind it.

The rhythm in every measure is the same — an eighth rest followed by five eighth notes. The seventh chord arpeggio sequences all take place on the top three strings, too, which is different from what you've played before. Keep your playing light to help the subdued melody show through.

Track 88

Bach and Gounod's "Ave Maria"

One of Bach's most famous compositions is his "Prelude No. 1" from *The Well Tempered Clavier*. It's a beautiful piece composed entirely of arpeggios. But 137 years after it was written, the French Romantic composer Charles Gounod came along and composed a melody to go on top of the chords. He called his mash-up "Ave Maria," even though everyone knew where he got the chords from.

The chords in "Ave Maria" change at the rate of one per bar, but the sequence is half a bar long, so each chord gets treated to two sequences. The arpeggio sequences presented in this piece are very close to those that Bach wrote. The pairs of sequences give the accompaniment a strong, predictable quality, yet it provides a subtle lift upward, capturing in this arrangement the ascendant quality of the original.

This piece almost begs to be played legato, so after becoming familiar with the arpeggio patterns called for in the music, try employing barres and held-down chord forms to make the notes ring out as long as possible.

Track 89

Part IV
Chords and Additional Exercises

"Shouldn't you be developing strength, speed, and independence on your guitar if not your life?"

In this part . . .

*I*f you want to take a breather from scales, arpeggios, and all that single-note playing, check out the material in the first chapter of this part, which deals exclusively with chords. Chapter 13 draws on chords as a way of helping you develop finger independence, but it also helps you increase your chord vocabulary in the process. Chapter 14 goes back to single notes and allows you to set your brain on autopilot while you just drill, drill, drill those fingers. The idea here isn't to think, but to take a simple finger exercise with no musically redeeming value and use it to build up strength and speed in your fingers. As Hans and Franz from *Saturday Night Live* might say, "Ve just vant to pump (*clap*) your fingers up!"

Chapter 13

Building Finger Independence with Chord Exercises

Chords are the rhythm guitar *yin* to the lead guitar *yang*. In most musical settings, single-note playing is supported by some sort of chord-based accompaniment. The great thing about the guitar is that it can play chords or single-note leads with equal awesomeness — try doing *that* with a flute or saxophone! But, because the guitar plays chords as well as single notes, it's important that you keep both your chording and melody skills up to snuff. The scales, arpeggios, and sequences described in Chapters 3 through 12 don't address chord playing in the way that this chapter does — with all the notes of the chord sounding *together*.

As is the case with the single-note exercises, the chord forms presented in this chapter are movable — meaning they contain no *open strings* (strings that are unfretted, with no left-hand finger touching the string at all). So after you can play a chord form comfortably, try moving it around the neck to play different chords. Doing this changes the letter name of the chord (for example, from A to C) but keeps the quality of the chord (major, minor, and so on) the same.

You can play the chords in this chapter a number of different ways with the right hand, including plucking the individual strings with your fingertips, brushing the strings with the backs of your fingernails, and striking the notes with a pick. But whether you pluck or strum with the right hand, your left-hand approach is the same. The fingers on your left hand must fret the notes in a way that allows the strings to ring clearly, and they must be able to change chords — that is, get off the old chord and grab the new chord — quickly and imperceptibly (or close to it, anyway). And this must all be done at a performance tempo.

The exercises in this chapter are designed to help get your fingers moving independently. The bountiful number of useful exercises also helps you build up strength in the process.

Practicing Inversion Patterns

Chords come in many different guises; even chords with the same name can be played in various ways. For example, you can play an F chord on the guitar in exactly one billion and seven ways. Okay, that's a *bit* of an exaggeration. But trust us, you can find lots of chord options on the neck.

The first way you can narrow down the F chord choices is to organize them by the low-to-high order of their notes. An F chord is spelled F-A-C, but the notes A-C-F and C-F-A are also F chords. Any chord with the combination of the notes F, A, and C constitutes an F chord, but if the lowest note of the chord is anything but an F, we call it an *inversion* of F. So we introduce you to an F (with an F on the bottom), its first inversion (with an A on the bottom), and its second inversion (with a C on the bottom).

In addition to the order of notes from bottom to top, you can also group chords by which strings they're played on. For example, you can play a chord using all six strings (as you do with a basic open E), just the top five strings, just the top four strings, or any other combination of strings.

Playing all six strings may make the guitar sound full and complete in one setting, but it's not always appropriate — especially if you're playing in a band or with other instruments. (Playing all six strings all the time can sound too full and can muddy up the texture and crowd out other instruments. It can be cumbersome to play, too.) Sometimes four-string chords are just right.

So here we employ two groups of four-string chords, nicknamed *outside chords* and *inside chords*. Outside forms refer to the top four strings that reach the outside, or edge, of the fretboard. Inside forms — at least for the purposes of this chapter (the term can have other meanings) — are the 2nd, 3rd, and 4th strings (which are insulated from the outside of the neck by surrounding strings) and a 6th string for a low note. Outside chords don't include bass notes, and they're good for supplying a higher harmonic part. Inside chords, which include a bass note, produce a deeper, fuller sound, and are good for when there's no bass player around.

Because we start our chord explorations at the 1st fret, we chose F to name our chords. But all of the forms presented in this chapter are movable, so when you practice playing them at different frets, the letter name changes. For example, if you play the chords two frets higher than where we present them in the figures, you produce G chords of various qualities. Our purpose in choosing F is that it's an efficient way to present all the different forms. But we don't favor F any more than G or B♭ or F♯. (Okay, maybe we like F a *little* more than F♯, but only because the key of F♯ has six sharps!)

As when practicing scales and arpeggios, play each chord exercise in this chapter slowly, loudly, and deliberately at first, making sure you can hear all the strings that are supposed to ring — and none of the strings that aren't! Then play the exercise faster and with a lighter touch. Just be sure to maintain your starting tempo and dynamic level (loudness) throughout each exercise.

Patterns using outside chords

The following figure shows the neck diagram and the corresponding music and tab for the three forms of an outside-string F major chord. Remember that when you practice these exercises, the *X*s in the chord diagrams mean that those strings aren't played. So avoid striking or plucking them with your right hand.

In all the rhythm examples that follow for outside chords, strum each chord lightly in quarter notes (one strum per beat) and avoid playing the lowest two strings of the guitar.

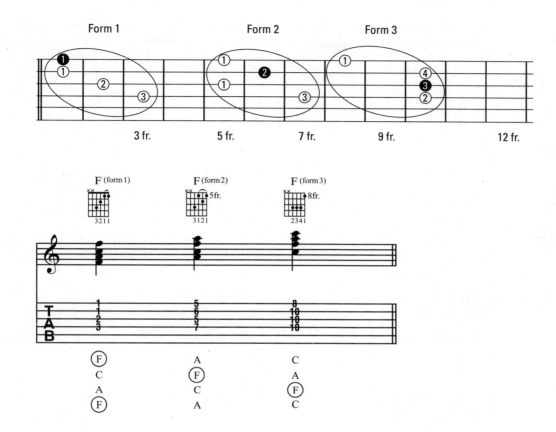

Now try the following exercise in rhythm, which uses the four outside forms of F, played two to a bar, or two beats on each chord.

When going from the first form to the second, keep your 3rd finger on the string as you slide up the neck. That way, you only have to reposition two other fingers (rather than all three). Apply the same "common finger" approach between the fourth and fifth chords in the exercise.

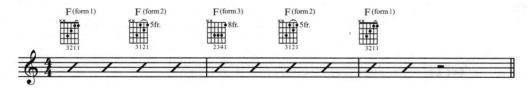

The following figure shows the neck diagram for the three forms of an outside-string F minor chord along with the corresponding music and tab. Practice this pattern as many times as you need to in order to play it smoothly — especially form 3, where you have to squeeze your fingers together a bit.

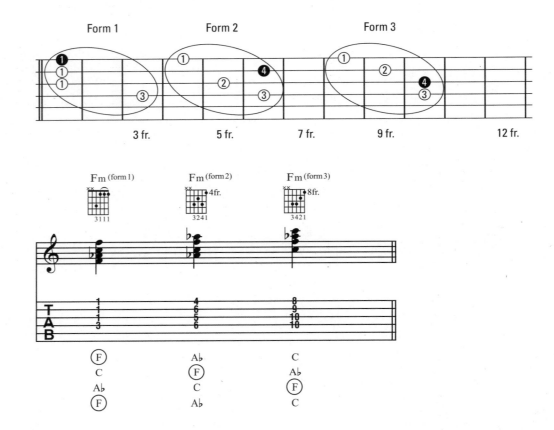

This exercise uses the four outside forms of F minor, played two to a bar, or two beats on each chord. The common finger approach that you use in the previous exercise works like a charm here: The 3rd finger plays the same string in all three chord forms. So keep it anchored on the 4th string as you move your hand up and down the neck.

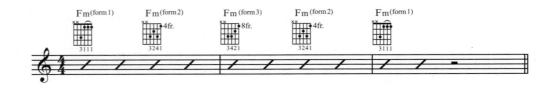

To see the neck diagram for the four forms of an outside F7 chord, along with the corresponding music and tab, check out the following figure. Practice the pattern here until you can move comfortably between the forms with no interruption in the rhythm.

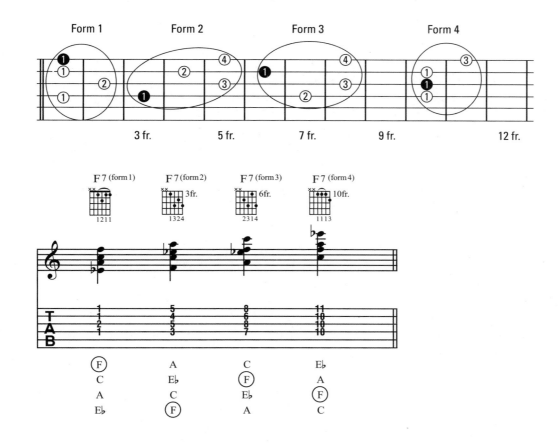

When you're ready, try the following exercise in rhythm. It uses the four outside forms of F7, played two to a bar, or two beats on each chord. Seventh chords are a favorite choice for blues rhythm players, so if you're interested, practice this progression with the additional blues chords of B♭7 and C7.

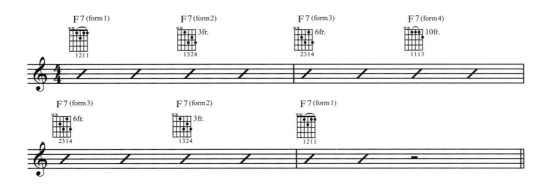

Now take a look at the neck diagram and corresponding music and tab for the four forms of an outside Fm7 chord. Try practicing this pattern in two ways: by playing it with a pick and by using just your right-hand fingers. Try to make the two approaches sound as close to each other as you can.

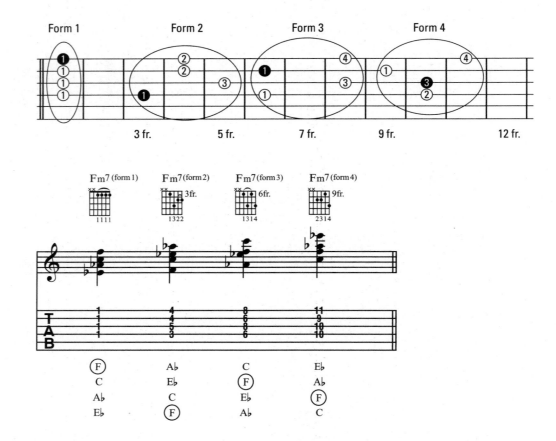

The following figure shows an exercise using the four outside forms of Fm7, played two to a bar, or two beats on each chord. Outside minor seventh chords are quite common in the jazz guitar style known as *chord melody,* so work for a smooth, even, and mellow sound as you play these chords. Imagine yourself jamming alongside a stand-up bass and a drummer using brushes.

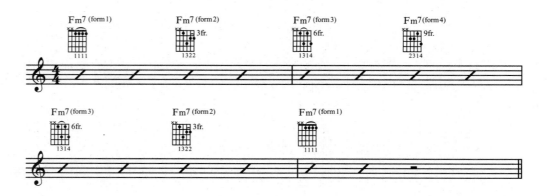

Here's the neck diagram and corresponding music and tab for the four forms of an outside Fmaj7 chord. Practice this pattern until you're completely comfortable with the four-fret spread among your left-hand fingers in form 3.

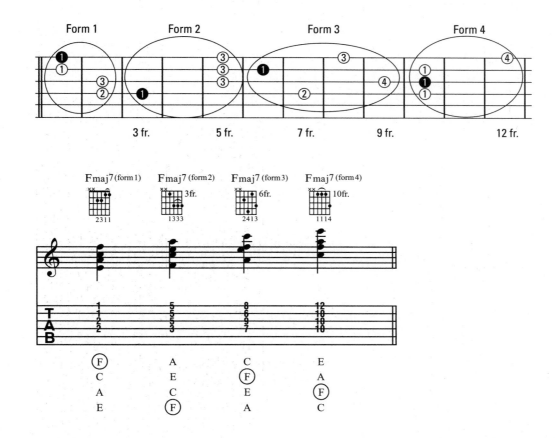

As practice, try the following exercise, which uses the four outside forms of Fmaj7, played two to a bar, or two beats on each chord. Form 3 is probably the trickiest chord in this series because it requires you to stretch your fingers out over all four frets in the position, and you have a wide space between the 2nd and 3rd fingers. Practice grabbing this chord in isolation (by removing your hand from the chord and replaying it several times) before playing the whole exercise up to tempo.

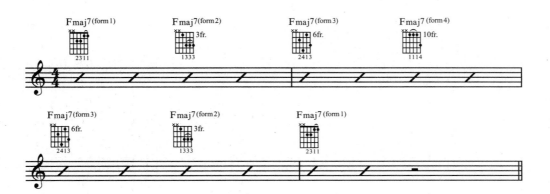

In the next figure, we show the neck diagram for the four forms of an outside F#m7♭5 chord along with the corresponding music and tab. Practice this pattern slowly at first and as many times as you need to until you have it memorized. Then, when you get "off book," work on playing it faster.

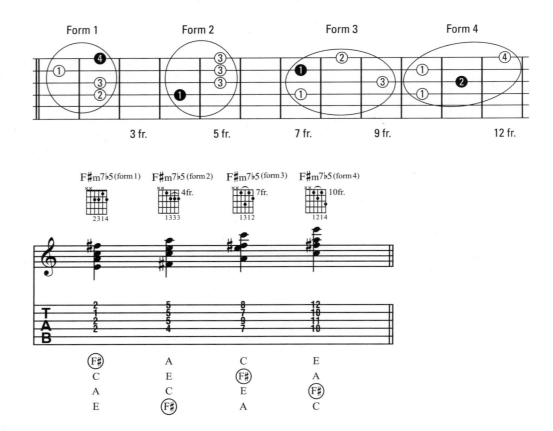

Now try your hand at this exercise, which uses the four outside forms of F#m7♭5, played two to a bar, or two beats on each chord. Except for the first and last chords, every chord in this exercise is played with a barre. Be sure to check your barre notes (by playing the individual strings one at a time, slowly) to make sure they're all ringing out clearly and with no buzzing.

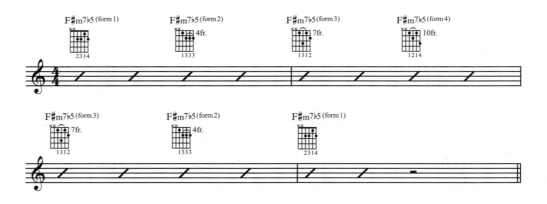

To see the neck diagram and corresponding music and tab for the three forms of an outside-string F#°7 chord, check out the following figure. Songs using the diminished seventh chord sometimes have you playing several forms in quick succession, so make sure you can play this at a fairly fast tempo.

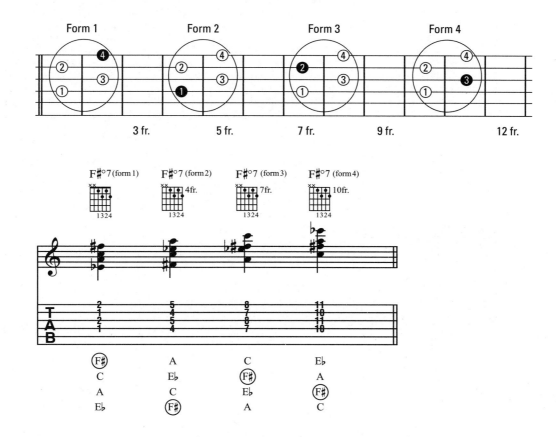

When you're ready to finish off your outside chord practice, take a look at the following figure, which shows an exercise in rhythm using the four outside forms of F#°7, played two to a bar, or two beats on each chord. The diminished seventh chord form has the same fingering for all of its inversions. So you get a free pass here and have to learn only one form, which you can slide up and down the neck with abandon. Because your fingers don't have to switch strings, try playing this example at a brighter tempo than you normally would.

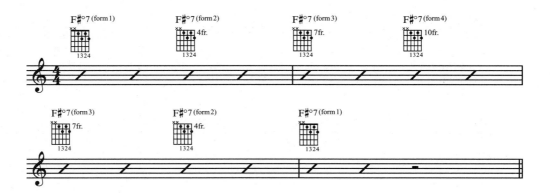

Patterns using inside chords

The following figure shows the neck diagram and corresponding music and tab for the three forms of an inside F major chord. Remember that the *X*s in the chord diagrams indicate that those strings aren't played. Practice this pattern as many times as you need to in order to get it to flow smoothly and so that there's no trace of that 5th string ringing through.

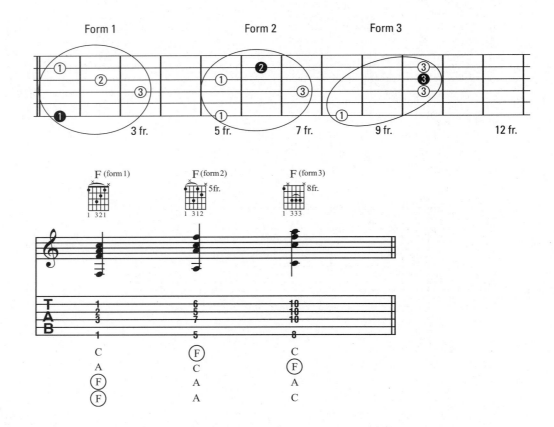

In the case of inside chords, it's difficult *not* to strike the 5th string when strumming (either with the backs of the fingernails or with a pick). So you should mute, or deaden, the string by allowing a left-hand finger to lightly touch it, which will prevent it from ringing out. This muting action is usually done by the finger that's fretting the 6th string. For the 1st string, simply relaxing the left hand so that the underside of the fingers touch the string lightly is enough to prevent it from ringing out.

You can practice this muting technique in the following exercise, which uses the three inside forms of F, played two to a bar, or two beats on each chord. Strum each chord lightly in quarter notes (one strum per beat), and avoid or mute the 5th and 1st strings of the guitar (indicated with *X*s in the chord diagrams).

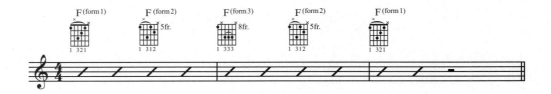

This next figure shows the neck diagram and corresponding music and tab for the three forms of an inside F minor chord. You can practice this pattern by keeping the 3rd and 1st fingers in the same basic shape as you change chords; they never leave the string they're on and they're always one fret apart from each other.

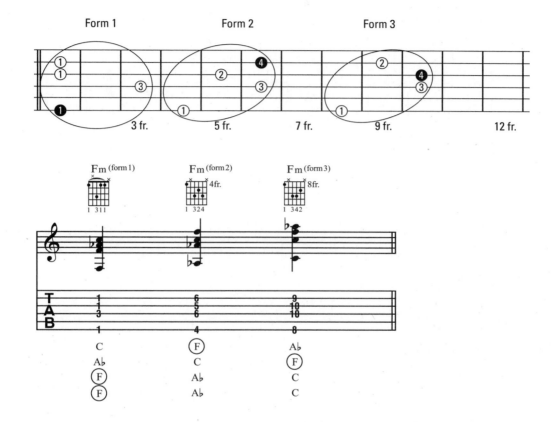

When you're ready, try the following exercise in rhythm, which uses the three inside forms of F minor, played two to a bar, or two beats on each chord. You may have trouble muting the 5th string on Form 1. So for this exercise, try plucking the strings with your right-hand fingers rather than strumming them with a pick.

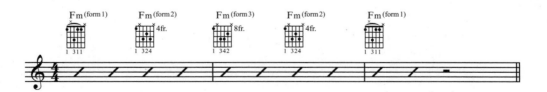

Now take a look at the neck diagram and corresponding music and tab for the four forms of an inside F7 chord. Make sure that you can blend all the notes together with your right-hand attack, and that no one note stands out above the rest. Practice this pattern so you can change smoothly between the chords that use barres (forms 1 and 4) and those that don't (forms 2 and 3).

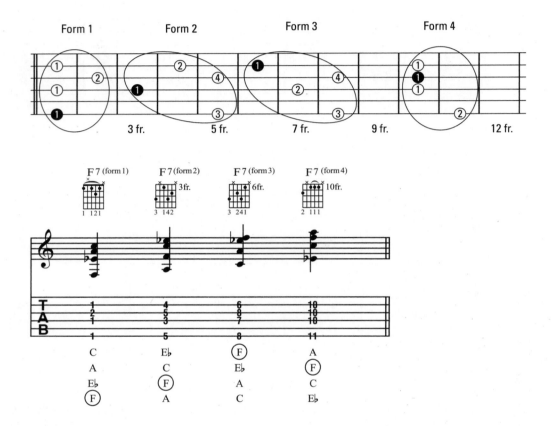

Give the following exercise a try. It uses the four inside forms of F7, played two to a bar, or two beats on each chord. Some guitarists, especially jazz players, like to use an alternate fingering for form 1. Try playing this chord with your 1st finger (not barred) on the 6th string, your 2nd finger on the 4th string, your 4th finger on the 3rd string, and your 3rd finger on the 2nd string. If you prefer this fingering to the barred version, you may be a jazzbo!

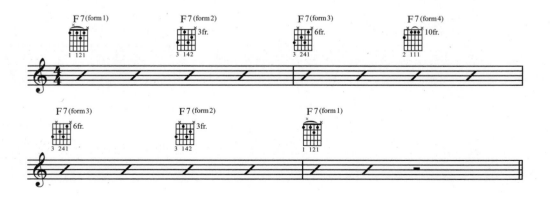

Here's the neck diagram and corresponding music and tab for the four forms of an inside Fm7 chord. Practice this pattern using two versions of form 1: the one indicated in the pattern, and an alternate form with the 2nd finger on the 6th string and a 3rd-finger mini-barre for strings 4, 3, and 2.

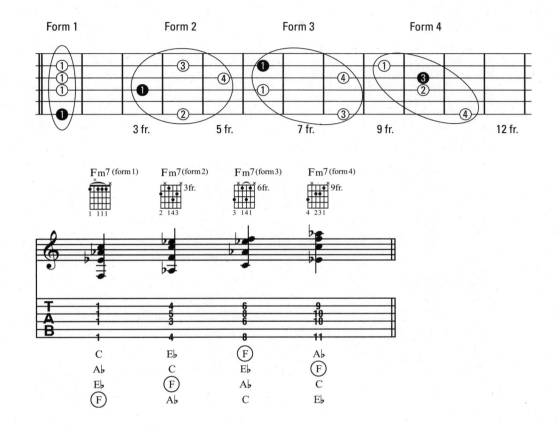

The following figure shows an exercise using the four inside forms of Fm7, played two to a bar, or two beats on each chord. Most experienced guitarists (jazz and rock players alike) play form 1 with the 2nd finger on the 6th string and the 3rd finger (barred) across the 4th, 3rd, and 2nd strings, as described earlier. Playing the chord this way helps you to better keep the 5th string from sounding. Try form 1 the two-finger way, and if it seems awkward at the 1st fret, move it up to the middle of the neck where it will be more comfortable.

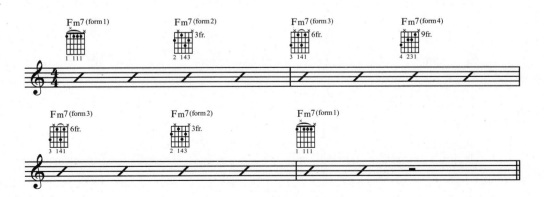

To see the neck diagram and corresponding music and tab for the four forms of an inside Fmaj7 chord, check out the following figure. Practice form 2 first in isolation because it has a stretch between the 2nd and 1st fingers. Then try the exercise in its entirety.

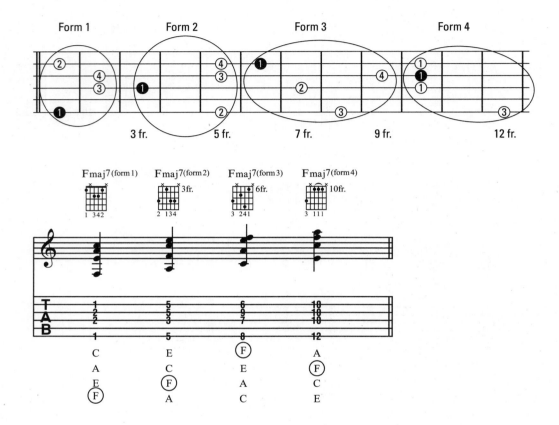

The following is an exercise using the four inside forms of Fmaj7, played two to a bar, or two beats on each chord. Between forms 3 and 4 you have an opportunity to make the chord change even smoother by leaving your 3rd finger on the 6th string as you move up and down the neck. Just be sure to relax the 3rd finger so it doesn't make a sliding sound on the string as you change positions.

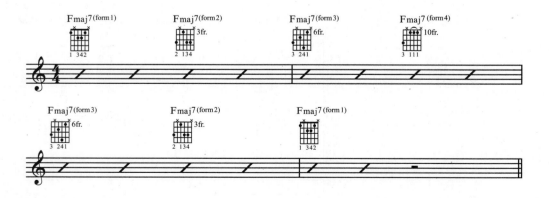

The next figure shows the neck diagram and corresponding music and tab for the four forms of an inside F♯m7♭5 chord. Practice this pattern several times or until you master the three mini-barres that occur in the exercise.

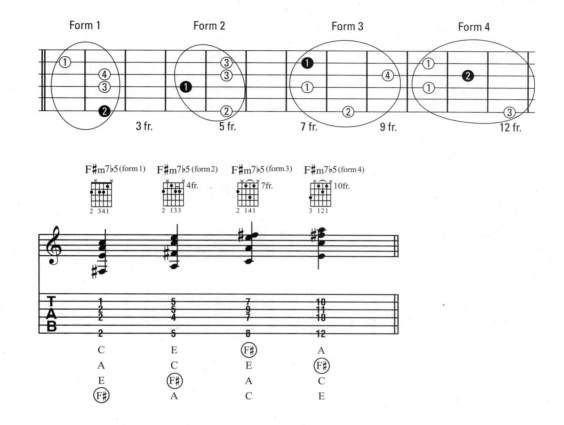

As practice, try the following exercise, which uses the four inside forms of F♯m7♭5, played two to a bar, or two beats on each chord. A very cool "common finger" chord change occurs between forms 2 and 3. Both the 2nd and 1st fingers stay on the same strings as they move to the new form. But the 1st finger goes from playing a single note on the fingertip to playing a barre on the flat part. So be sure to flatten out your 1st finger slightly as you move. To become familiar with this efficient finger movement, try isolating these two chords (that is, practice changing between the two forms a number of times before playing the whole exercise).

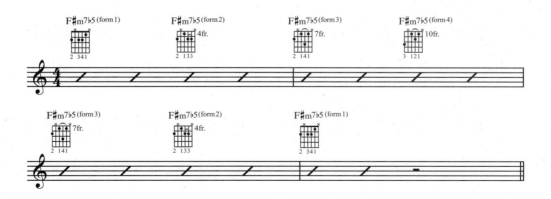

The following figure shows the neck diagram and corresponding music and tab for the four forms of an inside F♯°7 chord. Your fingering doesn't change when moving among the four forms here, so work for speed and accuracy as you shift this pattern up and down the neck in three-fret increments.

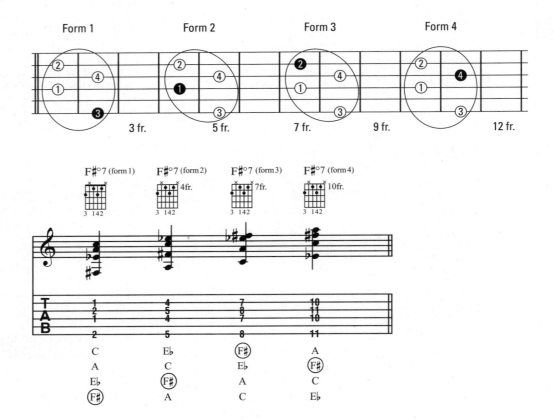

To practice, you can try the following exercise, which uses the four inside forms of F♯°7, played two to a bar, or two beats on each chord. Just as with the outside forms earlier in the chapter, the inside form fingerings of the diminished seventh chord are the same for all four forms.

 As if having the same forms didn't make things easy enough, we have another tip for you. Try the following alternate, three-finger version of the chord: Barre the 4th and 2nd strings with your 1st finger. Then play the 6th-string note with your 2nd finger and the 3rd-string note with your 3rd finger. Many guitarists find this fingering faster to grab than the one presented (especially after they become better at playing barre chords). Try both versions and decide for yourself, however.

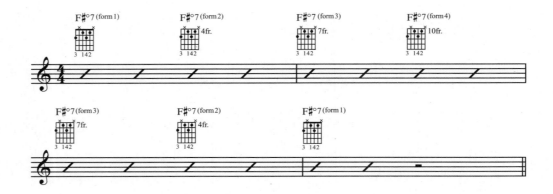

Playing Chord Progressions

Playing chords by themselves or organized by string assignment is a good way to get your fingers in shape. But in actual musical situations, you play chords according to another organizing principle: a chord progression. A *chord progression* is merely a series of chords that go together in a musically logical fashion — to support a melody or as the framework for a jam or improvisation (such as the 12-bar blues).

The chord progressions in the following sections may sound like real and familiar songs, and they should. That's because many songs have used the following progressions either in whole or in part.

Progressions using outside chords

Outside chord forms use the top four strings of the guitar (which are the highest pitched), and they're good for rhythm parts when you have a bass player in your midst (or when you're joined by a pianist who's playing low notes in the left hand). Outside chord forms are also nice when you want the brighter sound of the higher strings to cut through — the way a mandolin sounds when it plays rhythm.

The following figures show two chord progressions, each of which uses nine different outside forms, played two to a bar. Play the chord progressions both *legato* (letting the strings ring out as long as possible) and *staccato* (where the strings are muted by the release of your fretting fingers) to create two different moods.

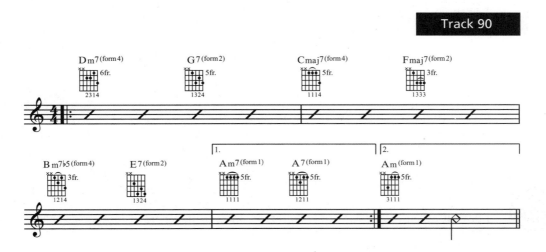

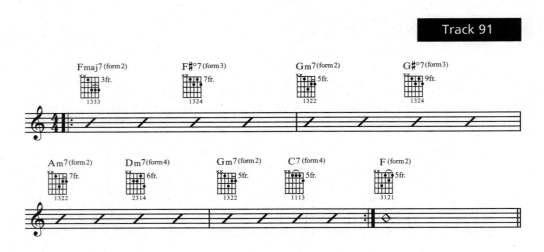

Progressions using inside chords

In this book, inside chords feature the 6th string as part of the chord, separated widely from the next highest note because of the skip of the 5th string. The presence of the low note in inside chords means that the inside chords provide a nice bottom, or bass part, which is good for solo guitarists, guitarists playing with other instruments but without a bass player, or accompanists backing a singer.

Take a look at the following figures, which show two chord progressions, each using nine different inside forms, played two to a bar. To help get the 6th-string note to ring a little more clearly, try separating it from the rest of the chord by plucking it a little harder than the rest of the strings. Or try playing the bass note with your right-hand thumb and the rest of the chord with your index, middle, and ring fingers. For extra practice, try playing just the bass note on beats 1 and 3 and just the upper three strings of the chord on beats 2 and 4.

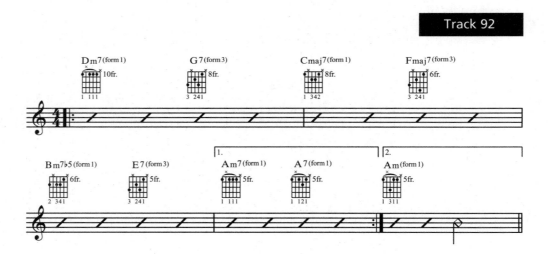

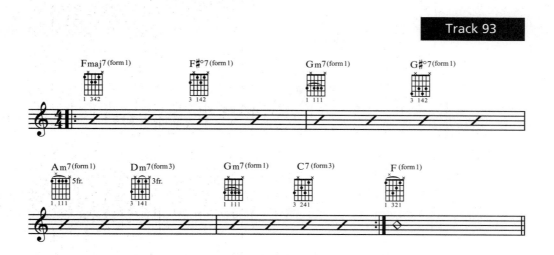

Track 93

Practicing Pieces That Use Chord Progressions

Seventh chords are great for playing jazz and jazzy types of arrangements, so we selected two songs to jazzify in the following sections: one is a traditional folk ballad and the other is a standard by Jerome Kern. The first song has you working with outside chords and the second one gives you an inside look at inside chords.

Putting outside chords to use with "Danny Boy"

The lovely Irish ballad "Danny Boy" is actually based on an old traditional melody called "Londonderry Air." And if you've ever checked out the *derrières* in London, you can see why they changed the title. *[Rim shot.]* The lyrics were added later, as a poignant message from a father to his absent son.

Play "Danny Boy" slowly and gently, and try to make the one-beat chord changes (which occur in bars 8, 9, 11, 12, 14, 15, and 16) sound smooth and unrushed. Don't worry if you can't play the F chord in bar 14 cleanly at first; it takes some effort to cram three fingers onto the 2nd, 3rd, and 4th strings all at the 10th fret.

You can try this alternate fingering if you're having trouble: Use your 3rd finger to barre the 2nd, 3rd, and 4th strings at the 10th fret, lifting it just enough to allow the 1st string (fretted by the 1st finger) to ring. It's tricky, but you may find it easier than using four separate fingers for this form so high on the neck.

Track 94

Moderately slow
Fmaj7 (form 2) 3fr. 1333
F7 (form 2) 3fr. 1324
B♭maj7 (form 4) 3fr. 1114
G m7♭5 (form 2) 5fr. 1333
Fmaj7 (form 2) 3fr. 1333
Dm7 (form 4) 6fr. 2314
Gm7 (form 2) 5fr. 1322
C7 (form 4) 5fr. 1113
Fmaj7 (form 2) 3fr. 1333
F7 (form 2) 3fr. 1324
B♭maj7 (form 4) 3fr. 1114
G m7♭5 (form 2) 5fr. 1333
Am7 (form 1) 5fr. 1111
Dm7 (form 4) 6fr. 2314
Gm7 (form 2) 5fr. 1322
C7 (form 4) 5fr. 1113
F (form 2) 5fr. 3121
Gm7 (form 2) 5fr. 1322
C7 (form 4) 5fr. 1113
F (form 2) 5fr. 3121
B♭ (form 1) 6fr. 3211
Am7 (form 1) 5fr. 1111
Dm7 (form 4) 6fr. 2314
Gm7 (form 2) 5fr. 1322
C7 (form 4) 5fr. 1113
F (form 2) 5fr. 3121
B♭ (form 1) 6fr. 3211
Am7 (form 2) 7fr. 1322
G7 (form 3) 8fr. 2314
C7 (form 1) 8fr. 1211
F (form 3) 8fr. 2341
B♭ (form 1) 6fr. 3211
G♯°7 (form 2) 6fr. 1324
F (form 2) 5fr. 3121
Dm7 (form 4) 6fr. 2314
G m7♭5 (form 2) 5fr. 1333
F (form 2) 5fr. 3121
Dm7 (form 4) 6fr. 2314
Gm7 (form 2) 5fr. 1322
C7 (form 4) 5fr. 1113
F (form 2) 5fr. 3121

Playing inside chords in "Look for the Silver Lining"

Jerome Kern wrote "Look for the Silver Lining" for an all-but-forgotten musical called *Sally,* but most people who know this call to optimism are familiar with the versions sung by Judy Garland or jazz trumpet great Chet Baker.

Play this song moderately slowly, and try to let the chords that last only one beat (such as the Am7 and D7 chords in bar 1) sound as legato as the chords that receive two beats.

The trick to this piece is making quick and efficient motions *between* chord changes without affecting the ring-out of the chord strums themselves. You need to change chords quickly, but you must also allow the chords to sound for their full duration.

Track 95

Moderately slow
Gmaj7 (form 1) Am7 (form 1) D7 (form 3) Gmaj7 (form 1) Gmaj7 (form 2) Cmaj7 (form 1)
5fr. 3fr. 5fr. 8fr.
1 342 1 111 3 241 1 342 2 134 1 342
Bm7 (form 1) Am7 (form 1) D7 (form 3) Gmaj7 (form 1) Em7 (form 2)
7fr. 5fr. 3fr.
1 111 1 111 3 241 1 342 2 143
3
Am7 (form 1) D7 (form 3) Bm7 (form 1) Em7 (form 4)
5fr. 3fr. 7fr. 8fr.
1 111 3 241 1 111 4 231
5
A7 (form 2) A7 (form 1) Am7 (form 1) D7 (form 3)
7fr. 5fr. 5fr. 3fr.
3 142 1 121 1 111 3 241
7
Gmaj7 (form 1) Am7 (form 1) Am7♭5 (form 1) Gmaj7 (form 1) Am7 (form 1) Am7♭5 (form 1)
5fr. 4fr. 5fr. 4fr.
1 342 1 111 2 341 1 342 1 111 2 341
9
Gmaj7 (form 1) G7 (form 1) G7 (form 2) C (form 1) E7 (form 3)
5fr. 8fr. 5fr.
1 342 1 121 3 142 1 321 3 241
11
A7 (form 1) A♯°7 (form 1) Bm7 (form 1) Em7 (form 3)
5fr. 5fr. 7fr. 5fr.
1 121 3 142 1 111 3 141
13
Am7 (form 1) D7 (form 3) G (form 1)
5fr. 3fr. 3fr.
1 111 3 241 1 321
15

Chapter 14

Developing Strength and Speed by Playing Single-Note Exercises

. . . .

In This Chapter

▶ Playing single notes across the neck

▶ Practicing single note moves along the neck

. . . .

*P*laying scales, arpeggios, and chords all involve some musical, as well as technical, consideration. That is, in addition to moving your fingers in time to the beat, you're also producing something that's musically meaningful — something that's heard in whole or in part in real songs and pieces. But what if you don't want to produce anything meaningful? Can you still accomplish anything with your guitar or should you just not play?

Actually, you're in luck. There's one instance where you can turn off your brain (at least the rational, thinking part), play something musically nonsensical, yet still be doing something productive. That instance is when you're playing speed drills and strength exercises. You can do these mind-numbing activities while watching TV, waiting for your computer to reboot, or waiting out a traffic jam (well, maybe not the last one, but you get the idea).

In this chapter, we present some technical moves that help you build speed, strength, and independence but won't tax your brain. In fact, you can just zone out like you would when distance running or weight training. You don't have to be thinking profound thoughts or figuring out how you're going to write the next great guitar solo.

For these exercises, you simply eyeball the patterns presented in the figures enough to learn them (we present these in a tab staff only). Then you kick back and let your fingers go to work while you give the old gray matter a rest. You just have to fill in the *etc.* instruction that comes at the end of each figure, because continuing in the same established pattern takes you to each exercise's logical end (the 12th fret for ascending parts and the 1st fret for descending parts). But otherwise, no thinking allowed!

Moving Across the Neck

In guitar-speak, moving *across* the neck means you go from one string to another while staying at the same position or fret number. For example, if you move your hand from the 6th string to the 1st string and back again — but you never let it stray from, say, the 2nd fret — you're moving across the neck. All the scales and arpeggios we explore in this book deal with moving across the neck. Even when you stretch to play an *out-of-position note* (a note that doesn't fall within the four-fret span defined by the position and that requires a stretch by the 1st or 4th finger to play it), you're still basically trying to preserve across-the-neck movement.

Moving across the neck to play different notes is a good way to execute a given musical passage, because you don't have to look at the neck to stay oriented (meaning you won't accidentally play bad notes!).

In the following sections, we introduce a series of exercises designed to build up your speed and strength, which keep you squarely in position while traveling across the neck. In these exercises, you change positions only after completing your journey from the 6th string to the 1st string.

Stepping up and down on one string

The exercises we provide in this section (shown in the following figures) all use a *stepping* motion, which means you play the frets in successive, numerical order (1, 2, 3, 4; 4, 3, 2, 1; etc.). In the ascending versions of these figures, you move across the neck going from the 6th string to the 1st string, and then you shift up one fret on the 6th string and begin the pattern again. Do this until your 4th finger reaches the 12th fret on the 1st string (that's what the *etc.* in the music is for — to remind you to keep going). ***Tip:*** You know you're on your last move across the neck when you start your 6th-string run at the 9th fret. For the descending versions, start with your 4th finger at the 12th fret and don't stop until your 1st finger hits the 6th string at the 1st fret.

We don't supply left-hand fingerings for these tab-only examples, but you can derive the fingerings for the ascending exercises from the tab numbers in the lowest position. For the descending versions, reverse the finger order. For example, if you play 1-2-3-4 for the ascending exercise, play 4-3-2-1 for the descending one. These exercises are easy to memorize, so work on getting them up to speed as soon as you feel you can go "off book."

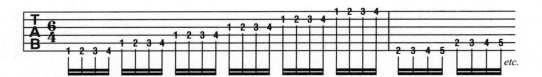

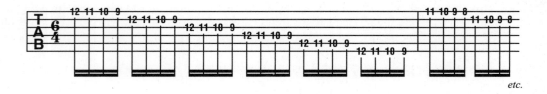

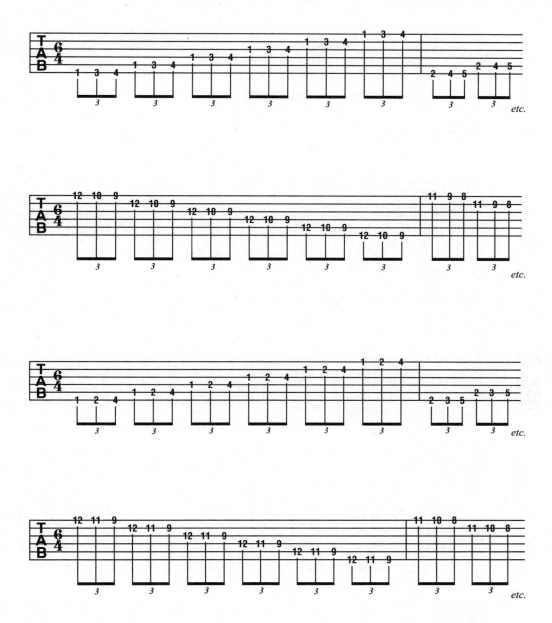

Skipping around on one string

The following figures all have one spot on each string where you don't play consecutive frets or use two adjacent fingers. In other words, you "skip around." Playing exercises like these that mix skips with adjacent-fret movements ensures that your fingers can "find" the frets even when the frets aren't right next to each other.

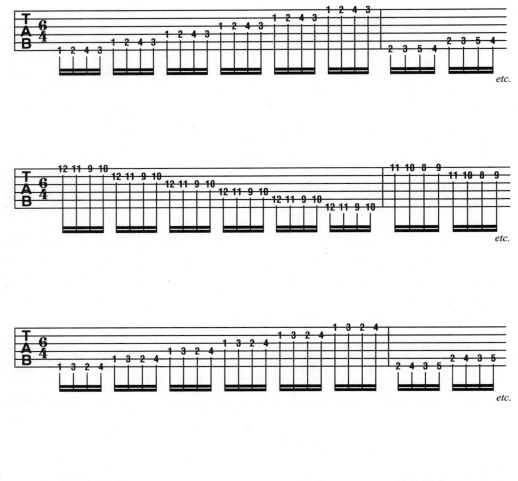

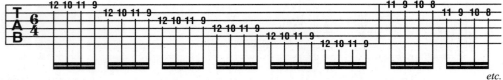

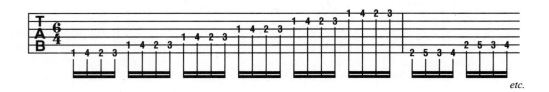

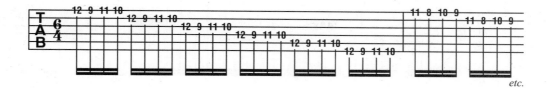

Jumping around on different strings

Tired of playing one string after another in predictable succession? Then you need to get some jump-time into your practice regimen! A *jump* is where you cross over to an adjacent string to play a given fret number. In other words, you still play the frets in sequence (that is, 1-2-3-4), but you alternate strings while doing so — playing the 6th string, 1st fret; then the 5th string, 2nd fret; then the 6th string, 3rd fret; and so on.

The following figures offer several different string-jumping exercises. If you play melodies with wide intervals or that change direction often, you'll be glad you practiced your jumping drills. Try lifting the previous finger at the same time you jump to the next note so you hear only one note at a time. This is good practice for *staccato* (detached, clipped) playing as well as for developing finger independence.

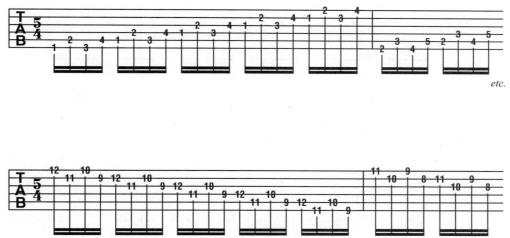

etc.

etc.

etc.

etc.

Moving Along the Neck

Moving *along* the neck means that you change positions — going from lower frets to higher frets, and vice versa, while playing. (Think of the word *along* and the fact that the neck is *long*.) Shifting your hand up and down the frets while remaining on one string moves you along the neck.

When you start moving up and down the neck, things get a little tricky. It's more difficult to move your hand along the neck and play accurately than it is to move across and play the correct notes. In moving along the neck, you can more easily play the wrong fret, or you can play the correct fret but not quite in the proper place, causing a buzz or muffled sound. Moving along the neck also requires that you look at your left hand while you play (unlike moving across the neck where you don't really need to look at all).

When you play chords and the chord exercises in Chapter 13, you get a taste of what it's like to move your hand up and down (or along) the neck. But we bring the concept of moving along the neck together with single-note playing in this next series of exercises.

Climbing up and down the strings

Climbing, as far as guitar playing goes, is the action of progressively moving up one string by starting a new series of notes at the next higher fret. For example, after you play frets 1-2-3-4 on the 6th string, the next note you play is fret 2 (on the 6th string) with the 1st finger — not the 2nd finger, as you normally would to remain in position. This allows you to gradually move up the neck, which is exactly what you do in this figure.

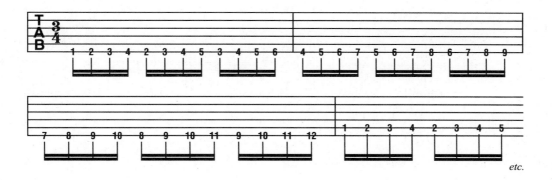

Now take a look at the following figures, which offer more variations for climbing up and down the strings. To increase efficiency and speed when descending, try placing all your fingers on the string at the same time, before you play the first note. Then simply peel off your fingers one by one, revealing the next, already-fretted finger.

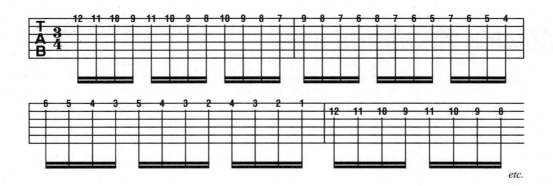

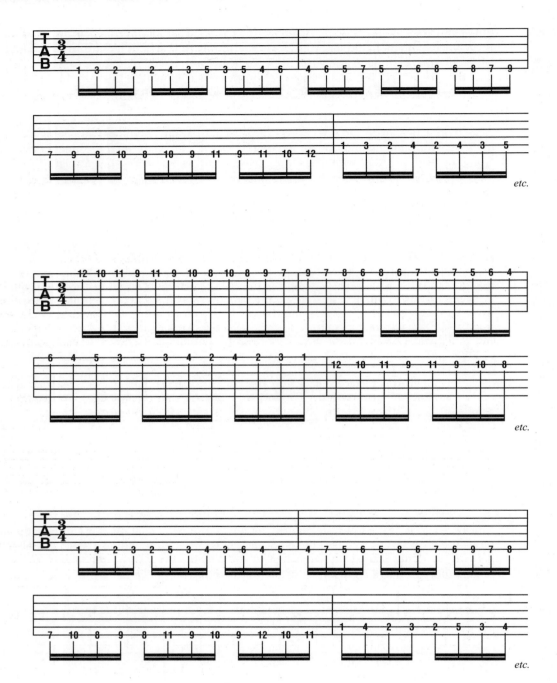

etc.

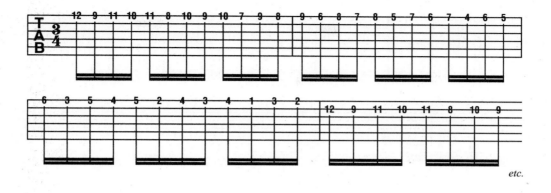

Ascending and descending with diagonals

Moving across the neck is fairly easy; moving along the neck is a bit more difficult. But hopefully you feel more comfortable doing both, because now it's time to combine *across*-the-neck moves with *along*-the-neck moves into *diagonal* movement. When moving diagonally, you play different strings *and* change positions — sort of like the guitar-playing equivalent of rubbing your stomach and patting your head, except that diagonal playing doesn't look nearly as silly. In fact, it's pretty cool once you master it.

The following group of exercises zig you and zag you around the neck with various ascending and descending diagonal patterns. Try to anticipate the shift by moving the finger that plays the next string in the new position as you play the last note of the current string.

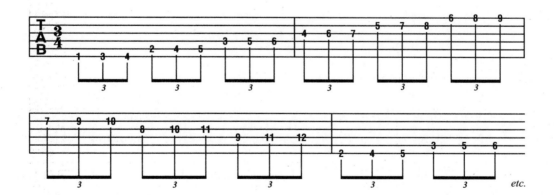

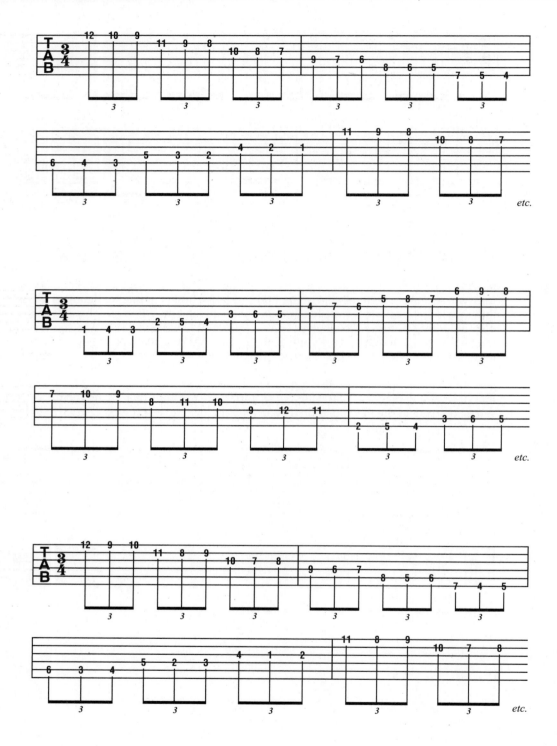

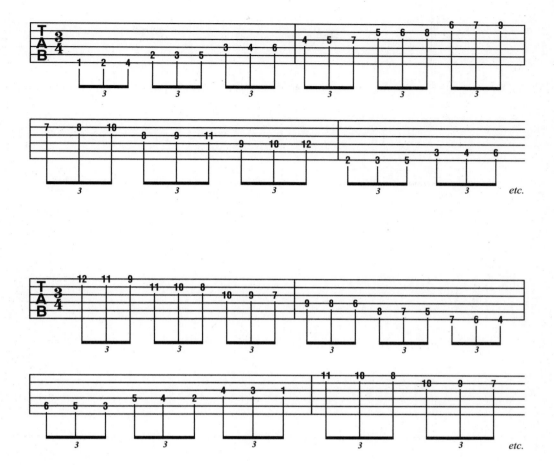

Part V
The Part of Tens

The 5th Wave   By Rich Tennant

"Practicing the guitar seems to have come very intuitively to her, unlike sitting on furniture."

In this part . . .

All *For Dummies* books — even one comprised entirely of exercises for the guitar — include a Part of Tens section. But we thought that instead of giving you ten additional exercises to practice (how predictable would *that* be?), we'd try to offer something a little different. We came up with two lists of things you can do that don't require you to run your fingers up and down the neck of a guitar ad infinitum. Chapter 15 provides some useful tips for maximizing your time with the guitar, and Chapter 16 lists ten important things you can do to improve your musicianship that *don't* involve playing scales, arpeggios, and chords on the guitar. Some of these activities, like watching and listening to guitar performances, don't require any work at all!

And don't forget the appendix, which gives a detailed rundown of the tracks on the CD as well as some instructions on how to use it — in case you haven't played a recording since 1982!

Chapter 15

Ten Tips for Maximizing Your Practice Time

Whether you have scads of time to practice or have to shoehorn precious musical moments with your instruments within a hectic schedule, your goal should be to maximize the efficiency of your practice time. Guitar playing is fun, but you improve your skills with practice and work. In this chapter are ten tips to satisfy your inner efficiency expert.

Establish Your Practice Place

Designate a practice space — one that's more or less permanent. Dedicating an entire room to music-making may be a luxury few people can afford, but that situation is ideal. Short of that, a corner of a room or a spot against a wall is the next best thing. In your practice space, you should devote a chair, a music stand, a good reading lamp, and a nearby table.

Define Your Practice Time (and Stick to It)

Ask anyone who has engaged in a successful exercise regimen, and she'll tell you that it's much easier to adhere to a routine if it takes place at the same time (or nearly so) every day. Practicing this way gives you an equal interval between sessions, and it lets you plan your life in advance. And so it is with music.

Establish Objectives for Your Practice Sessions

It's fun to just pick up the guitar and start playing, but you should save that for when it's *not* your scheduled practice time. When it's time to work, you should always begin with at least a goal or an objective (such as, "I'm going to learn three harmonic minor scale patterns and be able to play three sequences up to tempo"). These goals give you a way of measuring your progress.

Keep Your Accessories Handy

An *accessory* is any object you may need in order to practice comfortably and efficiently. Some important accessories include a metronome, tuner, pick (if applicable), and pencil and paper. You also may want to have a slide or digital memo recorder (for capturing ideas or monitoring your performance). But once you sit in your practice chair, you shouldn't have to get up again until the egg timer dings, indicating the end of the session. You may have to reach for something occasionally, but all the anticipated hardware you need to get through a session should already be there for minimum interruption.

Get Your Head in the Game

Approaching practice time with the proper attitude is something that's vitally important for productive results (and for simply remaining happier while you're in the chair). And it gets easier to do as you become better. But you'll likely find that even when you feel lousy, the mood disappears after a few moments of intense musical muscle-flexing.

Warm Up Your Hands and Fingers

Even if you're just bursting to play (having conquered the previous tip), you still have to wake up the muscles and nerves in your hands and fingers before they'll fire on all cylinders. Warming up with simple exercises allows your muscles to get in the groove without taxing your brain. And warming up prepares you for playing difficult passages better than if you simply try to stumble through them when you aren't quite ready.

Start Slow and Work Your Way Up

Many people don't realize the importance of playing a passage slowly and then speeding up gradually. Doing so not only helps diagnose where your weak spots are, but it's the most efficient way to get yourself playing up to tempo. Get out your metronome and find a comfortable tempo that's neither too slow nor too fast. After you can play the passage perfectly three times in a row, kick the metronome up one setting. Listen carefully for where the "breakdown" occurs. Usually, it begins in one or more specific spots.

Isolate Difficult Passages

You can isolate the passage that's dragging you down and practice just that bit, drilling just one or two bars over and over. Use your metronome to find the setting where you can play the difficult passage successfully and comfortably, and then work up from there. Be sure you can play into and out of the passage as well.

Play Different Guitars

You can get into a rut playing the same guitar. If you have more than one guitar, try playing your music on different instruments. This requires you to work the instruments a bit differently and to draw on different techniques to produce good tone.

Join the Club

Guitars sound equally fantastic in a solo or in an ensemble setting, so make sure you aren't just slaving away at home alone. Get out into the musical community and play with others! Try practicing duets with another guitarist, or experiment by backing up a singer. Then play in a trio, a quartet, or in larger settings, using both written arrangements and improvisation. You learn a lot about balancing and reacting dynamically. It's also a great way to get exposed to new points of view. Oh, yes, and it's fun too!

Chapter 16

Ten Ways to Improve Your Musicianship

We know it's hard to believe, but there are some things you can do to become a better musician that are *not* found in this book. Sometimes the skills for bettering yourself musically aren't instrument-specific. So, in this chapter, we offer ten ways you can improve as a musician without having to play scales, arpeggios, and chords.

Get with the Rhythm

Rhythm is the most basic force in music, and almost everyone can tap their foot or clap their hands to the beat. But you can go further in your pursuit of rhythm by identifying note duration values (quarter notes, eighth notes, triplets, sixteenth notes, and so on), understanding meters and time signatures, and sight-reading rhythmic notation in context and up to tempo. Doing these things gives you a much deeper appreciation for the beat than just "that thing you tap to." Recognizing rhythms helps you visualize what you hear and better memorize rhythmic figures and repeated rhythm patterns.

Familiarize Yourself with Pitch

The musical alphabet only goes from A to G, but it's the basis for your entire musical vocabulary. In fact, it's the basis for all things melodic and harmonic. Being able to name the pitches on the musical staff, guitar fingerboard, and piano keyboard increases your knowledge of the fingerboard and can help in scale construction, chord building, and sight-reading on the guitar.

Discover Harmony

Musicianship goes beyond rhythm and melody, and the next logical concept to tackle — especially for the guitarist who can play chords as easily as single notes — is harmony. Understanding how chords are built and recognizing the differences in their *qualities* (major versus minor, minor seventh versus dominant seventh, and so on) will help you recognize their sound and function in the music.

Perform Live for a Crowd

When you play live in front of people — either with other musicians or for an audience — you develop valuable skills that you just can't accomplish when practicing in private. Mustering your energy and marshaling your nerves in the right balance contributes to creating a potentially more powerful performance than you could achieve at home alone. Performing is just like any other skill: The more you do it, the better you become at it.

Compose Your Own Melody and Improvise a Bit

You may not (yet) be the next Paul Simon or Lennon and McCartney, but you should still try your hand at writing a song, composing a melody, and improvising over an accompaniment. Doing so taps different skills than simply memorizing music. You may not always produce something brilliant, but when you do spontaneously create something that works, it's a great feeling.

Train Your Ear to Hear

The concept of *ear training* involves aspects of the first three tips of this chapter (improving your rhythm, pitch, and harmony skills), but it applies to a broader strategy of getting your ears enrolled in a program of focused study. Ear training, under various names, is offered in all college-level music schools, regardless of your instrument. But you also can follow your own curriculum with individual study or with the help of a teacher or friend.

Polish Your Playing with Expression

Music isn't just about playing the correct note names precisely in the rhythms indicated. Music is ultimately an expressive act, so composers and performers also deal with *articulation* (how notes are struck or sounded) and *expression* (how music is performed). A good first step is being able to identify terms used to indicate expression (which are usually written in Italian) and symbols used to indicate articulation.

Listen to Lots of Music

Listening to music is what many people do for fun, but for guitarists, it's part of the job! (Aren't we lucky?) Listen to as much music as you can, especially in the style you're interested in learning. Be sure to listen critically, too. Try to identify the chords in the piece, the intervals in the melody, the instruments being played, and the techniques a performer uses to achieve a certain sound. Listening with a critical ear helps you develop your own sense of taste and solidifies your memory of the music and of that particular performance.

Watch a Performer's Body Language

Whether viewed on TV or from the fifth row in a concert hall (which is preferable, if you can afford it!), watch how performers play their instruments, hold their hands, move their bodies, and place their heads. Performing music is a whole-body experience, and you can often pick up good moves from watching great performers.

Test Yourself by Teaching Someone Else

Teaching is often a great way to gain perspective on what you think you already know. Having to show something to someone else often reveals gaps in your own knowledge, even if only for a moment. For example, you may know how to play a certain passage, but when your friend asks you to slow it down, you may find that you can't! It's a common phenomenon, but it forces you to rethink (and sometimes relearn) your approach to playing something. Taking what you know and presenting it to someone who's unfamiliar with that idea is a great way to cement your own knowledge.

Appendix

How to Use the CD

Guitar Exercises For Dummies is a true multimedia experience: You have text explaining the techniques, visual graphics of the music in several forms — chord diagrams, neck diagrams, tablature, and standard music notation — and audio performances of many of the music figures on your CD, complete with the appropriate accompaniment settings. With all those resources and this appendix as your guide, you'll be jamming in no time.

Always keep your CD with this book rather than thrown on your car seat or stuffed in a drawer somewhere. The plastic envelope helps protect the CD's surface from scuffs and scratches. Plus whenever you want to refer to *Guitar Exercises For Dummies*, the CD will always be handy. Also, try following along with the printed music whenever you listen to the CD, even if your music-reading skills aren't perfect. You absorb more than you expect just by moving your eyes across the page in time to the music, associating sound and sight. So make the CD and book constant companions, and use them together to help yourself better memorize and understand the music.

Relating the Text to the CD

If you're an experienced guitarist who's just looking for exercise routines, try reading through the music examples in this book and listening to the corresponding performances on the CD. If you want to dig deeper, read the text about each specific exercise or song. You may also want to go to a particular chapter or section that interests you (say, Chapter 8 on playing major arpeggio sequences), skip forward to the appropriate CD tracks, and play along. If the chapter you choose proves to be a little beyond your reach, simply go back to the chapter that starts the part (say, to Chapter 7 on playing major arpeggios) to see if that's more suited to your current level. Then you can work forward from there. As you can see, the modularity of this book makes finding what you need simple. And to help you out even further, the following sections show you some tips on finding and using the music examples on the CD.

Cueing up

You're bound to come across written music in this book that you want to hear or play along with. To listen to these pieces or examples on the CD, refer to the black box at the top of the figure, which tells you the track number and sometimes the start time (in minutes and seconds). Use your CD player's *track skip* control to go forward or backward to find the desired track, and then press play.

Count-offs, tuning, and metronome beats

All of the exercises in rhythm in this book begin with a *count-off* — a percussive click that acts as a metronome to establish the beat before the music begins. This count-off allows you to play the first note in time with the guitar that's playing on the CD.

Track 1 of the CD provides a tuning reference so you can tune up your guitar. The guitar on the recording plays the six open strings from low to high. Use your track skip function to replay the track until you have all six strings in tune with the CD.

The last four tracks, Tracks 96 through 99, have metronome beats at various tempos. Use these beats to practice the exercises at a progressive pace or to play along with any music you're working on where a metronome might be helpful.

Stereo separation

Some of the music that appears in this book is recorded in what's known as a *stereo split*. What we mean is that for the pieces that appear at the end of Chapters 3 through 13, the accompaniment appears on the left channel of your stereo and the guitar part appears on the right channel. If you have an adjustable *balance control* and leave it in its center position, you hear both the accompaniment and the featured guitar equally — one from each speaker. But by turning the balance knob to the left or right, you can reduce the volume of one part or the other.

Using stereo separation is important when you want to play along with the CD. Say you've practiced the guitar part to a certain piece and feel ready to try it "along with the band." All you have to do is turn the balance knob all the way to the left. By doing this you allow only the sound from the left speaker (the accompaniment) to sound. The count-off plays in *both* channels, so you'll still always receive your cue to play in time with the music.

Using the CD

The CD included with this book works just fine with any standard CD player. Just load it into the tray, and then press play or skip to the tracks you want to listen to and play along with.

You also can pop the CD into your computer's CD or DVD drive to access the tracks. However, first make sure your computer meets the following minimum system requirements:

- A computer running Microsoft Windows or Mac OS
- Software that's capable of playing CD audio (for example, iTunes, Windows Media Player, or RealPlayer)
- A sound card (almost all computers these days have the built-in ability to play sound)
- A CD-ROM or DVD drive

Tracks on the CD

Following is a list of the tracks on the CD. The track number is listed at the left and tells you what your CD player's display should read when you're searching for a particular figure. Scan through the descriptions to find the track you're interested in playing.

Track	*Description*
1	Tuning reference: the six open strings, low to high
2	Major scale pattern #1
3	Major scale pattern #2
4	Major scale pattern #3
5	Major scale pattern #4
6	Major scale pattern #5
7	"The First Noël"
8	Bach's "Minuet in G"
9	Major scale sequences using pattern #1
10	Major scale sequences using pattern #2
11	Major scale sequences using pattern #3
12	Major scale sequences using pattern #4
13	Major scale sequences using pattern #5
14	"Oh, Them Golden Slippers"
15	"We Wish You a Merry Christmas"
16	Natural minor scale pattern #1
17	Natural minor scale pattern #2
18	Natural minor scale pattern #3
19	Natural minor scale pattern #4
20	Natural minor scale pattern #5
21	Melodic minor scale pattern #1
22	Melodic minor scale pattern #2
23	Melodic minor scale pattern #3
24	Melodic minor scale pattern #4
25	Melodic minor scale pattern #5
26	Harmonic minor scale pattern #1
27	Harmonic minor scale pattern #2
28	Harmonic minor scale pattern #3
29	Harmonic minor scale pattern #4
30	Harmonic minor scale pattern #5
31	"God Rest Ye Merry, Gentlemen"
32	Handel's "Allegro"
33	"The Three Ravens"
34	Natural minor scale sequences #1 through #5
35	Melodic minor scale sequences #1 through #5
36	Harmonic minor scale sequences #1 through #5
37	"To Work upon the Railroad"
38	Bach's "Bourrée in E Minor"
39	"The Full Little Jug"
40	Major arpeggio pattern #1

Track	Description
41	Major arpeggio pattern #2
42	Major arpeggio pattern #3
43	Major arpeggio pattern #4
44	Major arpeggio pattern #5
45	"To the Colors"
46	"Retreat"
47	Major arpeggio sequences using pattern #1
48	Major arpeggio sequences using pattern #2
49	Major arpeggio sequences using pattern #3
50	Major arpeggio sequences using pattern #4
51	Major arpeggio sequences using pattern #5
52	"Blues Riff in B"
53	"Doo-Wop Groove in A"
54	Minor arpeggio pattern #1
55	Minor arpeggio pattern #2
56	Minor arpeggio pattern #3
57	Minor arpeggio pattern #4
58	Minor arpeggio pattern #5
59	"Wolfgang's Whistle"
60	"Amadeus's Air"
61	Minor arpeggio sequences using pattern #1
62	Minor arpeggio sequences using pattern #2
63	Minor arpeggio sequences using pattern #3
64	Minor arpeggio sequences using pattern #4
65	Minor arpeggio sequences using pattern #5
66	"Mozart's Motif"
67	Schumann's "Wild Horseman"
68	Dominant seventh chord arpeggio pattern #1
69	Dominant seventh chord arpeggio pattern #2
70	Dominant seventh chord arpeggio pattern #3
71	Dominant seventh chord arpeggio pattern #4
72	Dominant seventh chord arpeggio pattern #5
73	Minor seventh chord arpeggio pattern #1
74	Minor seventh chord arpeggio pattern #2
75	Minor seventh chord arpeggio pattern #3
76	Minor seventh chord arpeggio pattern #4
77	Minor seventh chord arpeggio pattern #5
78	Major seventh chord arpeggio pattern #1
79	Major seventh chord arpeggio pattern #2
80	Major seventh chord arpeggio pattern #3

Track	Description
81	Major seventh chord arpeggio pattern #4
82	Major seventh chord arpeggio pattern #5
83	Schubert's "Ave Maria"
84	Fauré's "Pavane"
85	Dominant seventh chord arpeggio sequences using patterns #1 through #5
86	Minor seventh chord arpeggio sequences using patterns #1 through #5
87	Major seventh chord arpeggio sequences using patterns #1 through #5
88	Liszt's "Liebestraum"
89	Bach and Gounod's "Ave Maria"
90	Outside chord progression #1
91	Outside chord progression #2
92	Inside chord progression #1
93	Inside chord progression #2
94	"Danny Boy"
95	"Look for the Silver Lining"
96	Metronome track #1: ♩ = 60
97	Metronome track #2: ♩ = 76
98	Metronome track #3: ♩ = 96
99	Metronome track #4: ♩ = 120

Troubleshooting

If you have trouble with the CD, please call the Wiley Product Technical Support phone number: 877-762-2974. Outside the United States, call 1-317-572-3994. You can also contact Wiley Product Technical Support at www.wiley.com/techsupport. Wiley Publishing will provide technical support only for installation and other general quality control items.

BUSINESS, CAREERS & PERSONAL FINANCE

Accounting For Dummies, 4th Edition*
978-0-470-24600-9

Bookkeeping Workbook For Dummies†
978-0-470-16983-4

Commodities For Dummies
978-0-470-04928-0

Doing Business in China For Dummies
978-0-470-04929-7

E-Mail Marketing For Dummies
978-0-470-19087-6

Job Interviews For Dummies, 3rd Edition*†
978-0-470-17748-8

Personal Finance Workbook For Dummies*†
978-0-470-09933-9

Real Estate License Exams For Dummies 978-0-7645-7623-2

Six Sigma For Dummies
978-0-7645-6798-8

Small Business Kit For Dummies, 2nd Edition*†
978-0-7645-5984-6

Telephone Sales For Dummies
978-0-470-16836-3

BUSINESS PRODUCTIVITY & MICROSOFT OFFICE

Access 2007 For Dummies
978-0-470-03649-5

Excel 2007 For Dummies
978-0-470-03737-9

Office 2007 For Dummies
978-0-470-00923-9

Outlook 2007 For Dummies
978-0-470-03830-7

PowerPoint 2007 For Dummies
978-0-470-04059-1

Project 2007 For Dummies
978-0-470-03651-8

QuickBooks 2008 For Dummies
978-0-470-18470-7

Quicken 2008 For Dummies
978-0-470-17473-9

Salesforce.com For Dummies, 2nd Edition
978-0-470-04893-1

Word 2007 For Dummies
978-0-470-03658-7

EDUCATION, HISTORY, REFERENCE & TEST PREPARATION

African American History For Dummies
978-0-7645-5469-8

Algebra For Dummies
978-0-7645-5325-7

Algebra Workbook For Dummies
978-0-7645-8467-1

Art History For Dummies
978-0-470-09910-0

ASVAB For Dummies, 2nd Edition
978-0-470-10671-6

British Military History For Dummies
978-0-470-03213-8

Calculus For Dummies
978-0-7645-2498-1

Canadian History For Dummies, 2nd Edition
978-0-470-83656-9

Geometry Workbook For Dummies
978-0-471-79940-5

The SAT I For Dummies, 6th Edition
978-0-7645-7193-0

Series 7 Exam For Dummies
978-0-470-09932-2

World History For Dummies
978-0-7645-5242-7

FOOD, HOME, GARDEN, HOBBIES & HOME

Bridge For Dummies, 2nd Edition
978-0-471-92426-5

Coin Collecting For Dummies, 2nd Edition
978-0-470-22275-1

Cooking Basics For Dummies, 3rd Edition
978-0-7645-7206-7

Drawing For Dummies
978-0-7645-5476-6

Etiquette For Dummies, 2nd Edition
978-0-470-10672-3

Gardening Basics For Dummies*†
978-0-470-03749-2

Knitting Patterns For Dummies
978-0-470-04556-5

Living Gluten-Free For Dummies†
978-0-471-77383-2

Painting Do-It-Yourself For Dummies
978-0-470-17533-0

HEALTH, SELF HELP, PARENTING & PETS

Anger Management For Dummies
978-0-470-03715-7

Anxiety & Depression Workbook For Dummies
978-0-7645-9793-0

Dieting For Dummies, 2nd Edition
978-0-7645-4149-0

Dog Training For Dummies, 2nd Edition
978-0-7645-8418-3

Horseback Riding For Dummies
978-0-470-09719-9

Infertility For Dummies†
978-0-470-11518-3

Meditation For Dummies with CD-ROM, 2nd Edition
978-0-471-77774-8

Post-Traumatic Stress Disorder For Dummies
978-0-470-04922-8

Puppies For Dummies, 2nd Edition
978-0-470-03717-1

Thyroid For Dummies, 2nd Edition†
978-0-471-78755-6

Type 1 Diabetes For Dummies*†
978-0-470-17811-9

INTERNET & DIGITAL MEDIA

AdWords For Dummies
978-0-470-15252-2

**Blogging For Dummies,
2nd Edition**
978-0-470-23017-6

**Digital Photography All-in-One
Desk Reference For Dummies, 3rd Edition**
978-0-470-03743-0

**Digital Photography For Dummies,
5th Edition**
978-0-7645-9802-9

**Digital SLR Cameras & Photography
For Dummies, 2nd Edition**
978-0-470-14927-0

**eBay Business All-in-One Desk Reference
For Dummies**
978-0-7645-8438-1

eBay For Dummies, 5th Edition*
978-0-470-04529-9

eBay Listings That Sell For Dummies
978-0-471-78912-3

Facebook For Dummies
978-0-470-26273-3

The Internet For Dummies, 11th Edition
978-0-470-12174-0

**Investing Online For Dummies,
5th Edition**
978-0-7645-8456-5

iPod & iTunes For Dummies, 5th Edition
978-0-470-17474-6

MySpace For Dummies
978-0-470-09529-4

Podcasting For Dummies
978-0-471-74898-4

**Search Engine Optimization
For Dummies, 2nd Edition**
978-0-471-97998-2

Second Life For Dummies
978-0-470-18025-9

**Starting an eBay Business For Dummies,
3rd Edition†**
978-0-470-14924-9

GRAPHICS, DESIGN & WEB DEVELOPMENT

**Adobe Creative Suite 3 Design Premium
All-in-One Desk Reference For Dummies**
978-0-470-11724-8

**Adobe Web Suite CS3 All-in-One Desk
Reference For Dummies**
978-0-470-12099-6

AutoCAD 2008 For Dummies
978-0-470-11650-0

**Building a Web Site For Dummies,
3rd Edition**
978-0-470-14928-7

**Creating Web Pages All-in-One Desk
Reference For Dummies, 3rd Edition**
978-0-470-09629-1

**Creating Web Pages For Dummies,
8th Edition**
978-0-470-08030-6

Dreamweaver CS3 For Dummies
978-0-470-11490-2

Flash CS3 For Dummies
978-0-470-12100-9

Google SketchUp For Dummies
978-0-470-13744-4

InDesign CS3 For Dummies
978-0-470-11865-8

**Photoshop CS3 All-in-One
Desk Reference For Dummies**
978-0-470-11195-6

Photoshop CS3 For Dummies
978-0-470-11193-2

Photoshop Elements 5 For Dummies
978-0-470-09810-3

SolidWorks For Dummies
978-0-7645-9555-4

Visio 2007 For Dummies
978-0-470-08983-5

Web Design For Dummies, 2nd Edition
978-0-471-78117-2

Web Sites Do-It-Yourself For Dummies
978-0-470-16903-2

Web Stores Do-It-Yourself For Dummies
978-0-470-17443-2

LANGUAGES, RELIGION & SPIRITUALITY

Arabic For Dummies
978-0-471-77270-5

Chinese For Dummies, Audio Set
978-0-470-12766-7

French For Dummies
978-0-7645-5193-2

German For Dummies
978-0-7645-5195-6

Hebrew For Dummies
978-0-7645-5489-6

Ingles Para Dummies
978-0-7645-5427-8

Italian For Dummies, Audio Set
978-0-470-09586-7

Italian Verbs For Dummies
978-0-471-77389-4

Japanese For Dummies
978-0-7645-5429-2

Latin For Dummies
978-0-7645-5431-5

Portuguese For Dummies
978-0-471-78738-9

Russian For Dummies
978-0-471-78001-4

Spanish Phrases For Dummies
978-0-7645-7204-3

Spanish For Dummies
978-0-7645-5194-9

Spanish For Dummies, Audio Set
978-0-470-09585-0

The Bible For Dummies
978-0-7645-5296-0

Catholicism For Dummies
978-0-7645-5391-2

The Historical Jesus For Dummies
978-0-470-16785-4

Islam For Dummies
978-0-7645-5503-9

**Spirituality For Dummies,
2nd Edition**
978-0-470-19142-2

NETWORKING AND PROGRAMMING

ASP.NET 3.5 For Dummies
978-0-470-19592-5

C# 2008 For Dummies
978-0-470-19109-5

Hacking For Dummies, 2nd Edition
978-0-470-05235-8

**Home Networking For Dummies,
4th Edition**
978-0-470-11806-1

Java For Dummies, 4th Edition
978-0-470-08716-9

**Microsoft® SQL Server™
2008 All-in-One Desk Reference
For Dummies**
978-0-470-17954-3

**Networking All-in-One Desk Reference
For Dummies, 2nd Edition**
978-0-7645-9939-2

**Networking For Dummies,
8th Edition**
978-0-470-05620-2

SharePoint 2007 For Dummies
978-0-470-09941-4

**Wireless Home Networking
For Dummies, 2nd Edition**
978-0-471-74940-0

OPERATING SYSTEMS & COMPUTER BASICS

iMac For Dummies, 5th Edition
978-0-7645-8458-9

Laptops For Dummies, 2nd Edition
978-0-470-05432-1

Linux For Dummies, 8th Edition
978-0-470-11649-4

MacBook For Dummies
978-0-470-04859-7

**Mac OS X Leopard All-in-One
Desk Reference For Dummies**
978-0-470-05434-5

Mac OS X Leopard For Dummies
978-0-470-05433-8

Macs For Dummies, 9th Edition
978-0-470-04849-8

PCs For Dummies, 11th Edition
978-0-470-13728-4

Windows® Home Server For Dummies
978-0-470-18592-6

Windows Server 2008 For Dummies
978-0-470-18043-3

**Windows Vista All-in-One
Desk Reference For Dummies**
978-0-471-74941-7

Windows Vista For Dummies
978-0-471-75421-3

Windows Vista Security For Dummies
978-0-470-11805-4

SPORTS, FITNESS & MUSIC

Coaching Hockey For Dummies
978-0-470-83685-9

Coaching Soccer For Dummies
978-0-471-77381-8

Fitness For Dummies, 3rd Edition
978-0-7645-7851-9

Football For Dummies, 3rd Edition
978-0-470-12536-6

GarageBand For Dummies
978-0-7645-7323-1

Golf For Dummies, 3rd Edition
978-0-471-76871-5

Guitar For Dummies, 2nd Edition
978-0-7645-9904-0

**Home Recording For Musicians
For Dummies, 2nd Edition**
978-0-7645-8884-6

**iPod & iTunes For Dummies,
5th Edition**
978-0-470-17474-6

Music Theory For Dummies
978-0-7645-7838-0

Stretching For Dummies
978-0-470-06741-3

Get smart @ dummies.com®

- **Find a full list of Dummies titles**
- **Look into loads of FREE on-site articles**
- **Sign up for FREE eTips e-mailed to you weekly**
- **See what other products carry the Dummies name**
- **Shop directly from the Dummies bookstore**
- **Enter to win new prizes every month!**